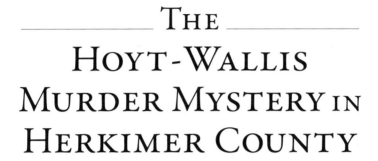

THE
HOYT-WALLIS
MURDER MYSTERY IN
HERKIMER COUNTY

JAMES M. GREINER

THE
History
PRESS

Published by The History Press
Charleston, SC
www.historypress.com

First published 2023

Manufactured in the United States

ISBN 9781467154888

Library of Congress Control Number: 2023935382

For Susan R. Perkins and Caryl Hopson

CONTENTS

ACKNOWLEDGEMENTS

In the spring of 1982, I was fortunate enough to be a guest of Madalyn Shoemaker Juna at her farmhouse in the township of Warren. The house had been in her family for three generations, and because of this, it resembled a museum. The parlor was adorned with numerous gilded framed photographs of relatives, while antique oil lamps (converted to electricity) cast a pale-yellow glow across the room. In the china cabinet were wedding dishes that belonged to her mother, grandmother and great-grandmother.

While sitting at the kitchen table, Madalyn entertained me with one story after another about her family's contributions to the history of Herkimer County, and before lunch was served, she went to the next room and presented me with an old scrapbook that had belonged to her mother, Alma. I had never seen a scrapbook quite like this one. While most scrapbooks contain personal family memorabilia, Alma's contained articles about some of her neighbors. In one clipping that described how a man struggled with a prolonged illness, Alma had written, "He was poisoned." In another, a story about a woman who had fallen into a well, Alma wrote, "She was pushed." If a barn burned, she wrote, "He set the fire."

Folded in the middle of the scrapbook was a May 11, 1901 issue of the *Saturday Globe*, featuring the Hoyt-Wallis murder. Until that moment, I had never heard of this Herkimer County murder. "You know," said Madalyn, "my mother always said he killed them both." Intrigued, I asked if I could have the paper.

Years later, I gave the newspaper to Susan R. Perkins, the executive director of the Herkimer County Historical Society. At that time, Sue was assisting me in researching my book *Last Woman Hanged: Roxalana Druse*, and I didn't have time to research another murder in the town of Warren. Once I finally had the time, together with Sue and her assistant Caryl Hopson, I gathered information about the Hoyt-Wallis murder, and they let me loose in the basement of the Suiter building to pour through period newspapers, several of which were invaluable to my research.

Period photographs are always welcome additions to books; however, the glass-plate negatives of the photographs that appeared in the *Saturday Globe* have long since disappeared. Fortunately for me, I was able to have the newspaper photographs reproduced for this book, thanks to the very talented Darryl Grubner.

Once more, I have relied on Patrick L. Kirk for legal advice. A big thank-you goes out to this old friend of mine for giving me a crash course in the divorce laws of the State of New York.

While visiting the "scene of the crime," I paid a visit to the clerk/register of vital statistics in the Town of Warren Anna Halkowich. As I suspected, there are times when the local vital statistics provide a little more information than what is provided by the state. The information she provided cleared up a few of the rumors surrounding the death of Ben Hoyt's wife and the cause of death of Jane Wallis.

Although Herkimer County does not retain the minutes from coroner inquests, it does have other materials that were important in my research. I am indebted to Debra Esty for retrieving the last will of Jane Wallis from the Surrogate records room. In the county clerk's office, Shirley Kuru and Emi Hall not only located several court cases involving John C. Wallis and his father, David, suing their neighbors, but they also located the *Wallis v. Wallis* divorce records.

Lastly, I have to thank my daughter, Beth, for her tech support (and her Microsoft Word cheat sheets) and my wife, Teresa, for her ongoing moral support and patience.

James M. Greiner

INTRODUCTION

In the mid-1880s, the township of Warren, nestled in the southern reaches of Herkimer County, was farm country. You either owned a farm, worked on someone else's farm or provided a service farmers relied on. Other professionals, such as carpenters, blacksmiths and even undertakers, provided services to those who worked the soil. There was no industry, and except for church and social gatherings, there was no way to keep abreast of the town's goings-on, as there was no newspaper.

In January 1885, the big story in Warren was the murder of William Druse at the hands of his wife, Roxalana. The volatile Druse marriage came to an abrupt end on December 18, 1884. That morning, an irate Bill Druse walked into the kitchen of his ramshackle farmhouse brandishing an axe. He accused his wife of chopping up one of his boards in the barn. Screaming at his wife, Bill thrust the axe into a cupboard door. While Roxalana sobbed hysterically, seventeen-year-old Mary Druse procured a .22-caliber pistol. Hiding the pistol in the folds of her dress, she passed it to her mother. Seated at the kitchen table with his back turned to his wife, Bill Druse remonstrated about an overdue store account. Roxalana fired off five shots in quick succession. Grievously wounded, Bill Druse slumped over the table. Mary took a dog leash, wrapped it around her father's neck and dragged him to the floor. Roxalana then retrieved the axe from the cupboard door and raised it above her head. "Oh, Roxy don't!" were the last words of Bill Druse. His severed head rolled aside as blood sprayed across the kitchen floor. Dragging the lifeless corpse into a side room, Roxalana and her daughter proceeded to dismember and burn it in a woodstove, while her nine-year-old son, George, and her thirteen-year-old nephew, Frank Gates, gathered wood shingles for the fire.

In the days that followed, Roxalana attempted to cover her tracks. She deposited the residue from the woodstove in a swamp and painted the kitchen floor. To inquiring neighbors, she said that Bill had gone to Little Falls and later to New York City. In an effort to make the latter more plausible, she produced a telegram that she had sent from Richfield Springs, urging him to return home. Neighbors didn't buy any of this. On January 13, Druse's next-door neighbor Charlie Pett went to Herkimer and expressed his concerns to District Attorney Abram Steele.

The next day, Steele arrived at the Pett farm and cracked the case in less than five minutes after interviewing Frank Gates. Following the coroner's inquest, Steele placed Roxalana, Mary and George Druse in custody, along with Frank Gates and his father, Charles. In April, the grand jury handed down indictments for murder against Roxalana and her daughter. George Druse and Frank Gates were released from the county jail when they agreed to testify against the two women. Charles Gates was released when Roxalana's accusations against him as the murderer of her husband were proved to be false.

The Druse trial ran from September 21 to October 6, 1885, and was front-page news across the state. Convicted of murder, Roxalana was sentenced to be hanged. After all her appeals had been exhausted, her spiritual advisor, Pentecostal minister Reverend George W. Powell, organized a letter-writing campaign and circulated petitions in an effort to convince Governor David B. Hill to commute her sentence. Governor Hill was unmoved, and Roxalana Druse was hanged on the gallows behind the Herkimer County Jail on the last day of February 1887.

The brutal kitchen murder of Bill Druse brought the tight-knit farm community of Warren unwanted and unpopular publicity. The "Druse murder," or the "Druse butchery," was bantered about by outsiders for years. It was a particularly heinous crime that residents wished outsiders would forget. In 1901, these same residents were shocked to learn that there was yet another kitchen murder that occurred in their township.

THE MARRIAGES OF TWO FAMILIES

L ike almost everyone else who lived in the vicinity of Van Hornesville, Thomas Tunnicliff could trace his family back to the colonial era. Family lore passed down from one generation to the next extolled the virtues and adventures of his distant relative John Tunnicliff of Derbyshire, England.

In a story that seems to be ripped from the pages of an old Hollywood script, John Tunnicliff, a landed aristocrat, allegedly killed a deer on his neighbor's land. Brought before the local magistrate, Tunnicliff was spared prison but not a stern lecture and hefty fine. The monetary loss was inconsequential. What irritated him was the scarcity of hunting land in his country and the steep taxes he was presently paying the British Crown. America, he believed, could provide him with the best of both worlds: more land to hunt on and fewer taxes.

Arriving in the colony of New York in 1756, Tunnicliff made his way into what is present-day Otsego County. Here, he discovered a wilderness of lush fauna, towering trees and picturesque lakes. Convinced he had found his Eden, Tunnicliff traveled by canoe to Albany and, after a meeting with land agents, purchased a tract of twelve thousand acres. Returning to Derbyshire, Tunnicliff spread the word from tavern to church, to family and friends. He was going back to America and welcomed anyone who wished to join him. The response was overwhelming. Tunnicliff had to charter his own ship and hire his own crew to make the return trip.[1] In the decades that followed, there wasn't a person in Derbyshire who didn't have a relative or a friend who had immigrated to central New York. By the 1850s, the Tunnicliff family tree had branched out like a mighty oak. In Van Hornesville, innkeeper Thomas Tunnicliff couldn't begin to name his second or third cousins. In the township of Stark, Herkimer County, which included Van Hornesville, the census enumerator recorded forty-six individuals who bore the name Tunnicliff. The same could be said of the neighboring township of Warren, which boasted forty-four more Tunnicliffs.[2]

As early as 1852, Thomas Tunnicliff was either contemplating or planning to move west. In that year, he sold a tract of land in the township of Stark to Charles Davy, and three years later, he sold another parcel to William M. Hosack.[3] The money generated from the sale of these properties may not have been enough to help him pay the mortgage on the inn that he shared with his wife, the former Jane Wigley. Living under the same roof were Jane's parents, William and Hannah Wigley, who had emigrated from, no surprise, Derbyshire, England. Joining his in-laws at the inn was his nineteen-year-old niece, Sarah Wigley, and his twenty-one-year-old brother, Jonathan C. Tunnicliff. Whether Thomas and Jane's decision to move west was based on finances will never be known. However, with so many family members living at the inn, one has to wonder how lucrative the innkeeper business was in this particular situation.

Before they packed a trunk, the decision to migrate west presented two problems. First, what was to become of the inn? When Thomas's younger brother Wellington stepped forward and offered to purchase the inn, Thomas was relieved, as the property would literally remain in the family. Wellington had married Jane's sister, Sarah. The second problem was of a more serious nature. What was to become of his wife's elderly parents? William and Jane Wigley had already made one great journey when they crossed the Atlantic in 1829. At the age of sixty-eight, William expressed no desire to begin life anew on the frontier. His sixty-four-year-old wife heartily concurred. Fortunately, the solution was near at hand. The couple would remain at the inn and be cared for by Thomas's cousin Joseph Tunnicliff, who just happened to be married to Mary Ann Wigley, another of Jane's sisters.[4]

At this time in American history, moving west didn't necessarily mean that you were going off to strike it rich in the gold fields of California. The arduous trek across the Great Plains and the Rockies by wagon train didn't suit everyone. Thomas Tunnicliff did not suffer from gold fever, but instead, he had caught a case of "Michigan fever." Throughout the 1850s, settlers, lured by cheap government land, migrated to the southern third of Michigan in record numbers.[5] Traveling west on the Erie Canal, migrants had only to board a packet boat on Lake Erie bound for the port city of Detroit. In no time at all, Detroit became the veritable Ellis Island of its day, as droves of "Yankees" and "Yorkers"—New Englanders and New Yorkers—arrived on the shores of Michigan to begin new lives.

Like many of the settlers who moved to Michigan, John and Jane Tunnicliff were neither rich nor terribly poor. With the sale of the inn, they realized they had enough money to make the journey and purchase land. Just as important, the couple had the advantage of knowing just where to go in Michigan. Another one of Thomas's wife's sisters, Margaret Wigley Baker, had been living in Kalamazoo County with her husband, William, since 1840.[6] Remaining with them for a short while, Thomas, Jane and their daughter, three-year-old Oretha, moved to the township of Portage. It was here that the former innkeeper turned pioneer purchased two hundred acres of land. By 1860, the labors of Thomas Tunnicliff were beginning to take shape. After clearing sixty acres of land, he set aside fields for crops and enough pastureland for cows, horses and sheep. While Oretha attended a one-room schoolhouse, Jane busied herself by maintaining the family's home and assisting with farm chores whenever she could. In 1863, the couple welcomed another daughter, Arvilla.[7]

Life on the Michigan frontier took a dramatic turn for the family in 1868 when Thomas died. His cause of death, as well as the exact date of his death, have perhaps been lost forever, as the small township of Portage kept poor records and had no newspapers at the time. What is known is that following her husband's burial, Jane had to do some serious soul searching regarding her future and that of her two girls. She and her husband had come to Portage with limited means and a dream. Through hard work and determination, they had built a good life for themselves. The death of her husband changed everything. Jane could not take on the responsibility of managing a farm and raising two children. There was only one thing she could do. After the funeral, she chose to sell the farm and move back to Van Hornesville. Surely, between her husband's many relatives and her own, there had to be someone who could help her in this, the most desperate time of her life.

In the spring or early summer of 1868, Jane and her two girls returned to Van Hornesville. Here, they reunited with family and friends who they hadn't seen in thirteen years. The hard times Jane experienced after the death of her husband didn't get any better when she returned to Van Hornesville. Finding a place to stay was fairly easy, as Tunnicliff homes and farms were strewn across the landscape in Stark and Warren Townships. Any number of these places would have put a roof over their heads. The problem Jane faced was how long she could stay at any one of these places. She didn't want to embark on a nomadic lifestyle, living in one place and then moving to another. It wasn't fair to her cousins, and it wasn't the best way to raise her two girls. She needed a permanent place. In the fall of that same year, fortune smiled on Jane. A widowed farmer by the name of Wallis in Jordanville was in need of a housekeeper.

Unlike the Tunnicliffs, David E. Wallis didn't have any deep family ties to southern Herkimer County. He was a native of Rensselaer; it was his wife's family who had settled had in the township of Warren. His wife's name was Sarah DeVoe, and it was her grandfather former Revolutionary War soldier Anthony DeVoe who had settled in nearby Andrustown in 1798.[8] Prior to the American Revolution, Andrustown was a small collection of farms scattered about the valley and hills less than fifteen miles from Fort Dayton in what is now the present-day village of Herkimer. These farms served as the "breadbasket" for the local militia groups, as every shed and barn had stockpiles of grain. On July 18, 1778, Mohawk chieftain Joseph Brant led a raiding party to Andrustown. In addition to killing three men working in the fields, Brant proceeded to torch every house and barn in the area. Andrustown never recovered and was never rebuilt. This, however, didn't stop men like Anthony DeVoe. He migrated from Rensselaer with the idea of farming the same fields that had been ravaged twenty years earlier. Over the next several years, more and more relatives who bore the DeVoe name settled in the same area.

For David and Sarah DeVoe Wallis, the road that led to the township of Warren took a slight detour. Arriving in Herkimer County in the late 1840s, David Wallis found work as a hired man on a farm in Paines Hollow, three and a half miles south of the Mohawk River. It was on this farm in 1849 that his wife, Sarah, gave birth to their first child, John. Three years later, a second child, David DeVoe, was born. By 1853, David E. Wallis had saved enough money to place a down payment on a farm one mile east of the village of Jordanville. The happiness the couple shared with the purchase of this new home was tragically short-lived, as that same year, the couple had to purchase a burial plot. One-year-old David was laid to rest at Highland Rural Cemetery. What the child died of is not known, and only a parent who has lost a child can fully comprehend what the couple endured. Each time they took the wagon into Jordanville, they passed by the cemetery, where they could plainly see the little headstone that marked the grave of their little boy.

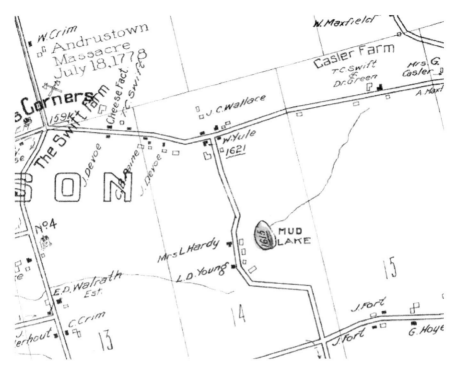

Note that the Wallis name is misspelled in this 1906 map. *From the* New Century Atlas of Herkimer County.

Like so many others who have experienced a personal loss of this magnitude, David E. Wallis coped by concentrating on the challenges presented to him each day on his farm. It was a comfort to him that his son was a constant presence at his side. While some children grew up with a pet name or family nickname, young John had to settle for going by his middle initial. From childhood to adulthood, he was always known as "John C." by his father. The father-and-son team worked tirelessly side by side, making improvements on the farm. With each passing year, the duo managed to clear more land and plant more crops. With the farm turning a profit, Wallis was able to hire seasonal workers. The hired men made life easier for the elder Wallis, as it then wasn't necessary for him to always be in the fields or in the barn, tending to a menagerie of animals. Farming required fieldwork and bookwork. With the farm economy as unpredictable as the weather, David Wallis, like most of his contemporaries, kept abreast of the latest market prices via the *Richfield Springs Mercury* newspaper or by discussing the local economy with fellow farmers while attending town meetings.

From the day he purchased his farm and before he even turned the first furrow of soil with his horse-drawn plow, David E. Wallis dreamed of adding more acreage to his farm. Over the years, Wallis stood by as the farm next to his changed hands several times. In those days, he didn't have the money he needed to make an offer on the property. In the summer of 1868, Wallis learned that his current next-door neighbor David Ward was contemplating moving to Columbia Center. Wallis saw his chance. The back-and-forth haggling between the two farmers that followed dragged on throughout the summer—and then it suddenly ground to a halt. Wallis had bigger problems at home that dwarfed negotiating a fair price for another farm. Since the spring, his wife, Sarah, had been in failing health. Throughout that summer, doctors tended to her while her husband looked on helplessly as her conditioned worsened. Suffering from complications of either consumption or cancer, Sarah DeVoe Wallis died on September 8, 1868. A friend of the family eulogized her: "Loving, affectionate and dutiful, she excelled in all that constitutes true womanhood, and her friends will realize her loss most deeply."[9] Forty-six-year-old Sarah was laid to rest beside her son David.

The loss of Sarah devastated David. The only reason he chose to settle in the township of Warren was because of his wife and her family. Now she was gone, and he didn't know what to do. Simply put, she ran the house, and he ran the farm. He and twenty-one-year-old John C. often worked from sunup to sundown, spending more time in the fields and barns than they did in their own home. What David Wallis needed was a full-time housekeeper. He needed someone who could cook, clean and, if need be, take the wagon to town to purchase necessary items for the house and farm. The offer wasn't all that appealing. Young girls didn't want to be tied down to a farmhouse doing chores. If they did, they would have married a farmer and had their own home to look after. By the same token, older women who had experienced this kind of work in the past wanted no part of it as they grew older.

Friends of David Wallis who sympathized with his plight spread the news from one farm to the next. Five miles away in Van Hornesville, Wallis learned that there was a widow who was interested in his offer. He immediately contacted her, and a few days later, she arrived on his doorstep. She introduced herself as Jane Tunnicliff. She had a bag in one hand, and in the other, she held the hand of her five-year-old daughter, Arvilla. Standing off to the side was sixteen-year-old Oretha. If Jane harbored any doubts about whether the girls would be accepted, her fears were quickly put at ease when David Wallis welcomed them into his home.

It's difficult to say who breathed the greatest sigh of relief. For Jane, it was as if a great burden had been lifted from her. Now, the forty-year-old widow did not have to face an uncertain future. She had a place to stay and didn't have to worry where her next meal was coming from because she would be preparing it. More importantly, she had the means to properly care for her girls. As for David and John C., their lives changed as well. After a long day of laboring in the fields, they no longer had to walk back to an empty house. The house was clean, the meals were prepared and their clothes were mended and washed. For David Wallis, the added bonus to having Jane as his housekeeper was the presence of Arvilla. The laughter and antics of the little girl changed the atmosphere of the house. The bleak, long days that followed the death of his wife, Sarah, had finally come to an end.

For Jane Tunnicliff, there was no doubt in her mind that she had made the right decision in accepting the position as the housekeeper on the Wallis farm. In the span of ten years, she witnessed the Wallis farm grow in size as well as wealth. On record, the farm had a value of $10,000. The thirty acres of tillable land produced cash crops of barley, buckwheat corn and potatoes. The thirty acres of pastureland were ample room for the farm's twenty-eight cows, half-dozen horses and flock of sheep, which could produce as much as sixty pounds of wool each year. At the same time, while many of the neighboring farms constructed "cheese houses" that helped Herkimer County earn the moniker "cheese capital of New York," Wallis chose not to get involved. Instead, he concentrated on producing milk and selling as much as four hundred pounds of butter a year.[10]

Another business venture Wallis shied away from was the hop industry. While neighboring farms were dedicating large tracts of land to cultivating this most necessary ingredient for beer, David Wallis didn't seem interested. The hop market was unpredictable to the point of becoming a gamble. There were just too many variables. Each issue of the *Richfield Springs* newspaper recorded the weekly update on the price of hops. Knowing the right time to sell was just as important as finding the right buyer. Next, there was the question of labor. A great many of the farms in the town of Warren placed advertisements in the Utica and Herkimer newspapers, looking for workers to pick hops. Since this was temporary work that lasted only a few weeks in the fall, it came as no surprise that many of the applicants were women. For David Wallis, this was simply out of the question. If you brought in extra help to pick hops, you had to not only feed them but also house them for the duration of picking season. The idea of selling hops and then paying temporary help whom you already housed and fed didn't add up to Wallis.

There were always the dangers of a bad crop, poor market value or both. He found another way to supplement his income, and it was physically effortless.

By the 1880s, neighboring farmers had begun referring to David and John C. Wallis as "wealthy farmers." The fact is that they were wealthy in land and liens. They spent some of their money wisely and invested the remainder of it carefully. Instead of depositing money that they had realized from their own physical labors in the bank, the Wallis men developed their own loaning institution. In true capitalist fashion, they used their money to make more money. For the next twenty years, father and son loaned money out to several neighbors' farms that experienced financial difficulties. In addition to these liens on farms, the two had no qualms about making personal loans. In either case, payments were due on time. For instance, in a case where blood was not especially thicker than water, John C. Wallis sued Wallace DeVoe for the repayment of a loan of $512. It didn't matter to John C. that DeVoe was his late mother's cousin. Wallis wanted his money, plus interest, and the Supreme Court of Herkimer County agreed with him. On September 9, 1897, John Wallis was awarded $698.66.[11]

As the country weathered the ups and downs of the agricultural economy, the Wallis farm remained solvent. The only major change that took place between the years 1881 and 1883 on the farm occurred when Davis E. Wallis abruptly fired his housekeeper. It wasn't that he was displeased with her work as much as he was displeased with himself. If anything happened to him, what would become of the woman who had become an important part of his life? In order to guarantee her future, David Wallis asked for her hand in marriage. The farmhouse Jane had tended for fourteen years was now her home.

2

ARVILLA

Wherever she went—and at whatever age—Arvilla Tunnicliff made quite the impression. "She was lively and happy in disposition," recalled a schoolmate, "and everybody loved her." The fact that she was well liked and well thought of was evident when hired man Norman Shaul's wife, Catherine, gave birth to a baby boy. He was christened "Arvillo."[12]

There was something special about Arvilla Tunnicliff. The day the five-year-old walked into the farmhouse was the same day she walked into the heart of David Wallis. A child's laughter hadn't been heard in the house for years, and he took to her immediately. "She was his ray of sunshine," recalled one neighbor.[13] Wallis doted on her as if she was his own little girl. Guiding her through her adolescent years was her mother. Having observed the lack of education exhibited by the hired men on the Wallis farm, Jane wanted better for her daughter. So, with the men tending to the fields, Jane looked after the house and made sure that Arvilla attended one of the several one-room schoolhouses in the township.

Although none of her school records—or anyone else's for that matter—still exist, it can be assumed by the letters she later wrote that she received a good education. She loved to read and was an accomplished organ player, and it was said she had a lovely voice. Just as important as the education she received at school was the socialization that came with it. On the Wallis farm, with its hired men, Arvilla was awash in a sea of adults. Her time spent in school gave her an education and a chance to socially interact with boys and girls her own age.

In 1880, one of the most popular girls in Jordanville was the free-spirited Arvilla Tunnicliff. *From the* Saturday Globe.

As a teenager, the once "pet of the neighborhood" had grown up to become "one of the belles of Warren."[14] She was intelligent, witty, beautiful and charming, and it certainly didn't hurt that she had, as one observed, "a good figure."[15] Arvilla Tunnicliff was one of the most sought after girls in the town of Warren. "Her heart and hand were sought by many a rural swain and, it might also be added, by many a city Romeo."[16] True, there were a few Romeos in the township of Warren, but as Arvilla was soon to discover, there were also the Capulets. After she finished school, Arvilla learned a hard lesson. Her destiny, it seemed, was tied irrevocably to the Wallis family.

Following her marriage to David E. Wallis, Jane became singularly obsessed with the future plans of Arvilla to the point of becoming an overly protective mother. Understandably, she simply did not want Arvilla to make the same mistakes as her older sister. Jane had lived on the Wallis farm for less than a year when her seventeen-year-old daughter, Oretha, suddenly announced that she was going to be married. Her betrothed was nineteen-year-old Almeron Brown. Jane may have opposed the match, but nonetheless, the two were married, and the following year, Jane became a grandmother. Her daughter and son-in-law, along with their infant boy John, settled in Burlington Flats in Otsego County. It was here that Almeron found employment as a hired man on a farm.

After ten years of marriage, Oretha obtained a divorce. Jane was horrified when she discovered that her oldest daughter, instead of returning to the Wallis farm for a brief stay, had pulled up stakes and returned to Michigan alone, leaving her ten-year-old son in the care of her ex-husband and ex-mother-in-law.[17] What went wrong or who was to blame for the failed marriage was difficult to explain. Jane probably reasoned it was a combination of several things that doomed the marriage. Not only was Oretha too young, but she had married too quickly. She had been in the Warren area for less than a year, hardly enough time to know you would want to spend the rest of your life with someone. And there was the possibility that Oretha had chosen the wrong man. Almeron Brown was a farm laborer, not a farm owner. Jane and her new husband, David, were determined that the judgmental mistakes made by Oretha would not be repeated by Arvilla.

As it turned out, the free-spirited—if not rebellious—Arvilla had ideas of her own. For the time being, life on the farm was tolerable. Assisting with farm chores and helping her mother in the house were expected, and she never complained. While Jane may have been well suited for this life, Arvilla did not look on this as her life's goal. All she had to do was look around the neighborhood. Not all of Arvilla's school friends remained on their families' farms. Granted, a few had walked down the church aisle and remained in town, but there were a handful of her friends who moved away from Warren. Some found work in the villages along the Mohawk River, while others went so far as to venture into the nation's larger cities.

At the age of sixteen, Arvilla had reason to believe that if she was going strike to out on her own, she better do it quickly. Throughout her teenage years, her mother gently teased her about John C. Wallis. Of medium height and sporting a Wyatt Earp–like moustache, John C., Jane believed, possessed all the qualities of a good husband. He was handsome, kind, hardworking and, because of his vast Wallis farm holdings, would be an excellent provider. In time, it became apparent to Arvilla that her mother was no longer dropping subtle hints. The gentle teasing of the "right man" turned into incessant nagging. Arvilla didn't mind having John C. as a stepbrother, but having him as a husband was out of the question. After all, there was quite an age difference—fifteen years.

While her mother and stepfather gently pressed the issue of marriage, Arvilla turned her attention to twenty-three-year-old Charlie Casler. He lived on his parents' farm one mile east of the Wallis place. With Charlie's help, Arvilla planned her escape. She would get to the Casler farm and then go off to the train station in Richfield Springs. It was of the utmost importance to get to the train depot, purchase tickets and immediately board the train. Arvilla didn't want to be sitting at the station for a long period. She wanted to be on the train, rolling down the tracks, by the time her mother discovered her absence. After reviewing the railroad timetable in the *Richfield Springs Mercury*, the two put their plan into motion. On the agreed-on date, Arvilla, having packed a trunk of her clothes and personal possessions, waited for the precise moment when her mother was out of the house. With her mother nowhere to be seen, Arvilla crept out of the house and loaded her things into a buggy. Confident that she had completed this undetected, she took the reins in her hands and gently steered the buggy in the direction of the Casler farm. When she arrived, Charlie was ready. He quickly off-loaded her belongings and put them in his wagon. The two had barely made their escape when from behind, they noticed a fast-approaching buggy. Apparently, Arvilla's escape from the farm had not gone unnoticed, as her mother and stepfather were in hot pursuit. David Wallis drew his rig in front of Charlie's wagon. He leaped from his buggy and approached the fleeing couple. Taking hold of Arvilla by the arm, he pulled her off the wagon seat. "He threatened the young man with prosecution," recalled one of Arvilla's friends, "and frightened him from the field."[18] Charlie Casler wasn't the only one "frightened from the field." Every boy in Jordanville and the vicinity of the Wallis farm got the message: stay away from Arvilla Tunnicliff.

After the failed wagon escape, Arvilla rarely ventured far from the farm, and when she did, it was always under the watchful eye of her mother. She did manage to attend a few social gatherings, and on March 20, 1884, she decided to host one of her own at Schoolhouse No. 5 in Jordanville. The party, according to the *Herkimer Democrat* newspaper, was "more than a success. Dancing was the order of the evening, good music helping in attendance. [A] princely repast was served at about eleven o'clock p.m., after which dancing resumed and continued until about four o'clock a.m., when the guests reluctantly dispersed, thanking 'Villa' for an evening of solid enjoyment."[19] Looking back, Arvilla probably had the feeling that the party was her last hurrah. For the rest of the summer, she was continually pressured by her mother to marry her stepbrother. "Her young companions," recalled one of her friends, "used to plague [tease] her about John, and often, she would burst into tears and sob as though her heart would break when the prospect of marriage with him was forced upon her."[20] Jane wanted her daughter to be financially taken care of, and at the same time, David Wallis wanted his son to marry the little girl who had walked into his home and heart all those years ago. At the end of the summer, Arvilla broke under the pressure and abided by her mother's wishes. On September 24, 1884, all four went to the Universalist parsonage in Richfield Springs, where Reverend Samuel R. Ward pronounced John and Arvilla husband and wife.[21]

After the marriage of his son, David Wallis and his wife took on the role of a retired couple. This was only made possible through the intervention of his son. Although his father was a spry seventy-three years old, John wanted

John C. Wallis at the time of his marriage to his stepsister. *From the* Saturday Globe.

him to slow down his pace of life. His days of plowing fields and cleaning out barns were over. Small chores that a hired man couldn't get to, like mending fences, was about all John allowed him to do. With his son running the farm and controlling the finances, the elder Wallis spent less time in the fields and barns. For the first time, he had the opportunity to do the things he wanted to do without having to worry about farm matters. Buggy rides to Van Hornesville to visit any number of his wife's Tunnicliff cousins and sisters were not uncommon.

In 1895, the Wallis men considered their futures and the future of their farm. The fact that David Wallis wanted his son to inherit the farm was never in question. The only problem was: who would inherit the farm from him? John

C. and Arvilla had been married for ten years and had no children. Father and son both knew that it was just a mere question of when they would have to sell the farm. They solved their dilemma in a unique way. On January 6, David and Jane Wallis, along with John C. and Arvilla Wallis, purchased a house in Richfield Springs. The plan was for David and Jane Wallis to move off the farm as soon as possible and take up residence in the village. For seventy-eight-year-old David Wallis and his seventy-one-year-old wife, Jane, trading the farm life for the village life of Richfield Springs was in their best interest. The village offered a multitude of stores and restaurants, but most importantly, especially at their age, it offered medical services. If and when the time came, the house would be passed on to John C. and Arvilla to be used as their retirement home.[22]

The plan of eventually moving to Richfield Springs did appeal to John C., but for the time being, retirement was most likely the last thing on his mind. As for his wife, Richfield Springs just wasn't her ideal big city. Until then, Arvilla had been content with her lot as a farmer's wife, performing the exact same tasks her mother had done for years in the Wallis home. Later, John C. recalled how Arvilla kept a meticulously clean house. In addition to keeping the house in order, she also tended to the chickens and churned butter. Any monies made from the sale of eggs and butter went to her purse. Her husband reasoned that this was only fair, as she was doing the work. This was a generous move on his part, as he had the reputation of keeping a heavy thumb on farm expenditures.[23]

Other than the purchase of the home in Richfield Springs, the only other significant event that occurred in 1895 on the Wallis farm was when a longtime employee suddenly quit. John C. Wallis never gave it a second thought when Ben Hoyt walked away from his farm. Hired hands came and went on large farms. Some drifted from one farm to the next depending on how much help was needed around the seasons they called spring planting and fall harvest. The only time a hired man stayed on for the winter was if the farm had a large herd of cows. In the case of the Wallis farm, which had no children to assist in farm chores, a hired man for the winter was a necessity. Feeding, milking the cows, cleaning out the barns and carrying out an assortment of odd jobs on the farm guaranteed a man room and board. In 1888, a hired man could expect to earn between twenty and twenty-four dollars a month; this included one day off a week and a primitive health insurance plan. If you were injured on the job, your employer was obligated to pay your doctor bill. Worse, if you died in a farmer's employ, they were obligated to bury you.[24] The work wasn't for everyone, but for unskilled men like Ben Hoyt, it was all they could expect.

Ben Hoyt was the oldest of eight children born to George W. and Martha Borst Hoyt. His father was a veteran of the Civil War and supported his large family as a stonemason in Vail Mills, a tiny hamlet outside of Mayfield in Fulton County. After receiving, at best, a rudimentary education, Ben Hoyt struck out on his own to make his way in the world. Unlike his father, who had acquired a skill, Ben, for the remainder of his life, was nothing more than a common laborer. Finding little work in Fulton County, Ben traveled to southern Herkimer County. It was in the township of Stark, the birthplace of his mother, that Ben Hoyt found work at the Borst farm.

Drifting from one farm to the next in search of better pay and accommodations was commonplace for any hired man. When Ben accepted a position on the Andrew Shaul farm, he became acquainted with their servant Mabel Hubbard. He took an immediate liking to her. While the two began a courtship, Ben continually sought higher-paying farm work. In late 1889, he began working full time on the Wallis farm. When he was not working on the Wallis farm, Ben crossed over a few fields and worked on the Ely farm. When the Elys needed more workers, Ben knew where to look. He encouraged his brother Andrew and his sisters Gertie and Rose to leave Vail Mills. Hired as part-time help on the Ely farm, the trio also became part-time help on the Wallis farm. Between the four of them, they thought they might be able to one day purchase the small Ely farm.

On August 29, 1893, Ben and Mabel were married in Richfield Springs.[25] Two years later, Ben abruptly walked away from the Wallis farm. While many speculated that Ben wanted to purchase the Ely farm, the reality was that his wife's health was not good. Her death on December 21, 1897, cast a cloud of suspicion over her husband.[26]

Rumors began to circulate throughout the township of Warren even before the first shovel of dirt passed over Mabel's coffin in the family plot at Roseboom in Otsego County. Her untimely death, some believed, could only be attributed to foul play. What people didn't realize was that Mabel didn't suddenly become ill, as she had been under a doctor's care for several weeks. It wasn't until December 10 that the doctors noticed the medicines they were prescribing had no effect on their patient. When she died, her cause of death was given as "peritonitis."[27] Although Dr. Henry R. Ward signed the death certificate, there were a great many people who had their doubts—so many that the body was later exhumed for a coroner's inquest. Not only did Mabel Hoyt suffer horribly from the effects of peritonitis, but the doctors noted that she had also been afflicted with "tubercular consumption."[28] The coroner's report, declared Jordanville resident W.W. Hill, "is a vindication of Mr. Hoyt, who has lived here for several years and who still remains here in his loneliness."[29] Despite this, the rumors persisted. "It was supposed," reported the *Little Falls Evening Times*, "she was poisoned, and her body was exhumed, but no evidence was obtained on which the authorities could fasten a crime to anyone."[30] Suspicion regarding his wife's death dogged Ben Hoyt for the rest of his life.

SCANDAL IN JORDANVILLE

In 1898, the Board of Charities for the State of New York noted that the only charitable institution in Herkimer County was the Old Ladies' Home in Mohawk. Established in 1895, the Victorian-style brick mansion housed homeless women and elderly women who found it physically or financially impossible to remain in their own homes. The staff who looked after the dozen or so women could be best described as housekeepers. If one of the elderly women became ill, she was transferred to a hospital. Retirement homes of this nature were found in cities and small villages such as Mohawk. In a rural setting, the best a widowed old lady like Margaret Yeomans could hope for was family to tend to her needs during her twilight years.

Born in 1803 in England, Margaret was most likely descended from the Wigley family. Little is known of her early life, but at the age of sixty-seven, she was a boarder in the home of Joseph and Mary Wigley Tunnicliff in the township of Stark. She remained here for ten years, and after that, she later lived in the homes of several of her nieces. In some instances, she would reside with them for a year, and at other times, she would remain for only a season. During the winter months of 1897, "Old Auntie" Yeomans was a guest of David and Jane Wallis. After the snow melted, she moved back to Stark to live with Adelbert and Charlotte Tunnicliff.[31] The following winter, Old Auntie returned to the Wallis farm. As a caregiver, Jane Wallis did everything in her power to ensure that her elderly aunt was comfortable. Bedridden and in failing health, Margaret Yeomans died on March 3, 1898, at the age of ninety-four. Her funeral was attended by many, and she was eulogized as a woman who "was respected by all who knew her."[32]

Being a caregiver had taken its toll on Jane's health. The months of caring for her aunt had left her, as her doctor said, with "low vitality and general prostration." A much bigger concern to her doctors was her irregular breathing. On April 1, four weeks after the death of her aunt, seventy-four-year-old Jane Wallis succumbed to pneumonia.[33]

The loss of Jane left David inconsolable. The retirement home that he and Jane had planned to move to was now nothing more than another piece of property. Thirty years previously, he had opened the front door of his home and ushered in Jane and her two girls. He never really got to know Oretha, but Jane and Arvilla made his house a home. While David Wallis saw to the funeral arrangements, his son and daughter-in-law made their way by horse and buggy to the nearest telegraph office. In Richfield Springs, Arvilla waited patiently as the telegrapher tapped in Morse code, "Mrs. Oretha Crain Yorkville Michigan."

Following her divorce from Almeron Brown, Oretha returned to Michigan. Two days before Christmas 1885, Oretha Tunnicliff Brown married again. The thirty-three-year-old joined hands with the recently widowed James McElroy, a fifty-one-year-old farmer from Kalamazoo. McElroy was much wealthier than Oretha's first husband. He wasn't a hired man on a farm; instead, he owned the farm. In addition to farming, McElroy had diversified interests. He was selling stock, raising crops and dabbling in real estate. This union lasted until McElroy's death on April 2, 1892, after a prolonged illness. On August 15, 1894, Oretha said "I do" for the third time when she accepted the hand of her neighbor, Alfred Crain, a former business acquaintance of her late husband. As with her previous marriage, there was quite an age difference between the spouses. He was fifty-nine years old, and she was twenty years his junior.[34]

On Sunday, April 3, 1898, a melancholy David Wallis stood by the grave of his first wife, Sarah, and watched as the undertakers lowered the body of his second wife into her grave. It is doubtful Oretha was able to arrive in time for the service, but when she did appear, she spent about a week going back and forth from the Wallis farm to Van Hornesville, visiting cousins she hadn't seen in thirty years.[35] One could only surmise what occurred at the reunion between Oretha and her son John. The little boy she had abandoned when she moved to Michigan was now a married man. As it turned out, Oretha didn't have to look all that far to find him. John had recently married Ella McRorie and was currently employed on the Wallis farm.[36]

The stories Oretha told her sister about her life in Kalamazoo were certainly pleasant to listen to, but then again, the setting was a farm. By this time, Arvilla had grown weary of the rural life and longed for something new and exciting. Reality, as we know, quickly replaces daydreams. Her entire world was the Wallis farm, and it got a little larger with the death of her mother. It was one thing to do the cooking and cleaning in her own home, but now she was expected to do the same for her father-in-law. Arvilla may have viewed herself as a prisoner on the farm, unable to leave due to her housework and other duties. However, her husband certainly didn't feel the same way. John C. could come and go as he pleased, and he often did. Working and managing the accounts for two farms took up almost all of his time. As he learned from his father, only certain jobs could be assigned on the farm. It was common practice to send a man to Jordanville or even to the train stations in Little Falls or Richfield Springs to collect supplies. However, settling accounts in stores and collecting money were different matters. With liens and loans spread across the township of Warren, father and son called on farmers to collect on their accounts that were due. They were not miserly bill collectors, however. The Wallis men believed people should be given a chance, especially if they had fallen on hard times. A perfect example of this generosity could be seen when Ben Hoyt asked to be rehired. Following the death of his wife, he was financially unable to purchase the Ely farm.

Bringing Ben Hoyt back to the farm didn't present any immediate problems. Already familiar in the Wallis way of doing things, Ben didn't have to be told what to do twice. Arvilla, too, was happy to have Ben back on the farm. They were close in age, enjoyed each other's company and easily shared their feelings concerning the loss of loved ones. As the months went by, townspeople who passed by the Wallis farm could often see Arvilla leaning out the western downstairs window, chatting with Ben. However, after two years had passed, some neighbors had good reason to believe that they were much more than "good friends." Their relationship was, as one newspaper recalled, "the gossip of the neighborhood."[37]

While some were convinced that Arvilla and Ben were intimate, others could not believe that John C. was oblivious about what was taking place. John C. had a good idea what was happening. On March 23, 1899, his suspicions were confirmed when he arrived home unexpectedly and discovered Arvilla and Ben in his bed. What happened next was incredible. Not only did he not begin divorce proceedings against his adulterous wife, but he also didn't fire Ben Hoyt. The only thing John C. Wallis did was move to another bedroom in his house and, as he later said, "not voluntarily cohabitate" with her.[38]

For John C. Wallis, a divorce was simply more embarrassing than practical for him. What would the townspeople say? The image he and his father had cultivated as respected members of the community would come into question. A divorce would forever cast him as a man who could not control his wife. For the time being, Wallis chose to do nothing. In his naiveté, he believed, things would, in time, sort themselves out. As for Arvilla, she should have been thankful that her husband didn't file for a divorce. If he had, she would have been homeless with no means of supporting herself. Her only option would have been to bring her tarnished reputation to Stark and beg from her Tunnicliff cousins. Instead, she decided to vanish.

In the early evening hours of September 9, 1899, John C. Wallis made his way back home from the fields and knew something was wrong the minute he entered his house. Not only was the oil lamp unlit, but the cookstove was cold to the touch. After lighting the lamp, he made his way slowly upstairs and gently pushed the unlatched door to Arvilla's bedroom aside. A casual glance around the room by the light of the lamp was all he needed. There was no bedding, no clothes, no rug and no Arvilla. Returning downstairs, Wallis entered the small bedroom off the kitchen. In the corner of the room was a small safe with its door left ajar. An envelope containing $1,200 was missing. Wallis closed the safe door and pondered his next move. It was too late to go looking for Arvilla, and it was useless to try to find Ben Hoyt.

The following day, Wallis walked across the road to the Willard Yule farm and asked questions. Had anyone noticed anything unusual at his place the day before? Willard wasn't much help, but his wife, Minnie, noticed something peculiar. The previous afternoon, Minnie Yule told Wallis, she saw a horse and buggy by his barn. A woman wearing a black dress exited the barn and got into the buggy. The driver of the buggy, she recalled, sped off rather quickly in an eastern direction on the Jordanville Road. To Wallis, this could only mean the pair was going to a railroad station in Little Falls. He then asked if Minnie had caught a glimpse of who was in the buggy. Minnie said that was strange, as she couldn't recognize anyone because the curtains were drawn. She didn't understand why anyone would do this, as "the day was bright and pleasant."[39]

A smartly dressed Ben Hoyt poses for the camera sometime before he and Arvilla fled to Michigan. *From the* Saturday Globe.

Returning home, Wallis hitched his horse to a buggy and proceeded east, stopping at farms along the way to make discreet inquiries. Assisting him was one of his mother's DeVoe cousins and neighbor Perry A. Wood. Well aware of the problems Wallis was having in his marriage, Wood wasn't at all that surprised to learn that Arvilla had run off with Ben Hoyt. While Wood canvassed the farms closest to the Wallis farm, John C. drove east, and after passing the Casler farm, he turned the buggy left onto Hicks Road. When he reached the Hoke farm, he spoke with Nicholas Hoke and Rollin Zoller. Both were positive they had seen the buggy Minnie Yule had described.

There were several livery stables in Little Falls, and Wallis had a hunch that Ben had rented the horse and buggy from the stable closest to the railroad station. He was right. Edward V. Decker operated Sales and Stables at 320 South Second Street, a block away from the New York Central and Hudson River Railroad station. Decker told Wallis that he didn't know Ben Hoyt, but someone who matched his description did rent a horse and buggy from him the previous day. Whoever this person was, Decker said, brought the rig back to his stables sometime between 4:00 and 5:00 p.m. And yes, added Decker, there was a woman in the carriage wearing a black dress.[40] After making inquiries at the ticket office and baggage station, Wallis learned that Arvilla and Ben had boarded a westbound train. He had no doubt in his mind that the pair was going to Michigan.

In retrospect, Wallis had to begrudgingly give Arvilla credit for a well-executed flight. Obviously, she and her paramour had been planning their escape for several weeks. Wallis later learned that Ben Hoyt had tried to sell his horse to one of the local farmers. Hoyt told Richard Luther that he needed the money because he planned to run away with Arvilla. At first, Richard Luther thought Hoyt was joking. Luther later recalled telling Hoyt, "John C. would be on their tracks." Hoyt didn't appear to be concerned. He told Luther that he "didn't care a damn for John C." When Hoyt produced a wad of bills from his pocket, Luther changed his mind.[41] As for Arvilla, he deduced that her trunk full of clothes had been placed in the barn the previous day. While he was tending to morning chores, she was stripping the bed and taking the pillows out to the barn. When Ben Hoyt arrived with the buggy, all he had to do was pull the rig close to the barn, pack up her belongings and then make his escape. By the time John C. returned from the fields, Arvilla and Ben had already boarded their train. The timing couldn't have been better.

While Arvilla and Ben made their way to Michigan, John C. turned his buggy around and made his way to Herkimer. As far as he was concerned,

Arvilla had committed moral suicide by running off with Ben Hoyt. By now, she was miles away, unable to hear the vicious gossip that was being bantered about, but her husband wasn't. He still lived in the township of Warren. For Wallis to save face in the community, he had to obtain a divorce as quickly as possible. His reputation in the community was at stake.

For his representation, John C. Wallis opted for one of the oldest law firms in Herkimer, the Prescott and Steele Law Firm located in the Fox building on Main Street. After entering the building, Wallis introduced himself to William C. Prescott. A native of New Hartford, Prescott had attended local schools in Utica and furthered his education at Tufts College. After graduation, he studied law, and after passing the bar in 1875, he partnered with Robert Earl and, later, Sam Earl. When the Earl brothers left the firm to pursue political ventures, Abram B. Steele came on board.[42]

When Wallis gave a brief synopsis of his dilemma, Prescott appeared unmoved. A hired man running off with the boss's wife was nothing new in Herkimer County. Six years earlier, on August 26, 1893, William Carmine, a farmer from Fairfield, arrived home after traveling to Little Falls to collect groceries, only to be informed by his son that his wife had run away with their hired man. Carmine immediately went to the train station in Little Falls and confirmed that his wife, Mary, and Arthur Putnam had purchased a ticket and boarded a train bound for Syracuse. "We have been married fourteen years," howled the clueless Carmine, "and this is the first shadow that has come over our home."

Arvilla and Ben Hoyt were much better at running away than Mary and Arthur Putnam had been. Arvilla made a clean break due to good planning. Not only did she know where she was going, but she had a substantial amount of money as well. Mary Carmine's flight had a spur-of-the-moment quality to it, especially when Arthur Putnam had the audacity to wire her husband from Syracuse asking for ten dollars.[43]

Prescott informed his client that no matter what he had heard about divorces, it was difficult but not totally impossible to obtain one in the state of New York. Since the late 1700s, the only grounds for filing a divorce in the state was adultery. Although several measures had been introduced in the state legislature to amend the existing divorce laws—such as a spouse being absent for five years—none had been passed by the legislature. Still, Prescott said there were other ways to secure a divorce. In some instances, aggrieved spouses simply needed to move to a neighboring state to take advantage of their more liberal divorce laws.[44] Wallis said it was highly unlikely Arvilla would divorce him, because she didn't have the means. Prescott understood and told Wallis that his task was twofold: not only would he have to prove to the court that his wife was an adulterer, but he would also have to secure sworn statements from his neighbors to back up his claim of her infidelity and make a more serious effort to locate his errant wife. Once these things were accomplished, he could begin "divorce by default" proceedings. This, Prescott explained, could only take place when the accused, Wallis's wife, could not be located to be served with divorce papers.

Upon his return to Jordanville, Wallis went right to work by immediately confronting his hired man. John Brown said he had absolutely no idea where his aunt Arvilla was, but he did have the address of his mother in Yorkville, Michigan. Wallis wasted no time in dashing off a short note to Oretha. Several weeks later, he received a reply. As he suspected and expected, Oretha claimed that she hadn't seen her sister and had no idea where she might be. Wallis wasn't naïve. He knew she was lying. After all, where else would Arvilla go? The only thing that was important to him now was that he had the written proof his errant wife could not be located.

On October 16, 1899, Wallis, in the company of Perry A. Wood, met with William C. Prescott. Presenting Prescott with the letter from Oretha Crane, Wallis signed a sworn statement about the events leading up to and details about his wife's infidelity, plus his failed attempts in locating her. The statement Perry A. Wood signed focused on how he had searched for Arvilla and Ben the day after their disappearance. After both statements were notarized, Prescott told Wallis that before the end of the day, the papers would be on the desk of County Judge Irving R. Devendorf.[45]

After a brief consultation with Prescott, Judge Devendorf agreed that a divorce was justified. The statements made by Wallis and Wood were, as Devendorf said, "proof to my satisfaction that the defendant has departed from this state or keeps herself concealed therein to avoid the service of a summons." He then ordered that the summons for Arvilla to appear in court be published in both Herkimer newspapers, the *Herkimer Democrat* and the *Herkimer Citizen*, "once a week for six consecutive weeks."[46] If, at the end of the six weeks, Arvilla still could not be located and served a summons, then the divorce case would be entered into the court calendar.

4

WALLIS v. WALLIS

At the turn of the twentieth century, divorce trials in major cities were major events. This was the era of yellow journalism. Spawned by the likes of newspaper moguls William Randolph Hearst and Joseph Pulitzer, sensationalist reporting was the rule of the day. Nothing garnered larger headlines and beckoned more readers than a high-society divorce fraught with philandering husbands, cheating wives or both. As divorce trials were open to the public, courtrooms were often standing room only as men and women eagerly listened to all the juicy details of infidelity. Thankfully for John C. Wallis, the local press wasn't swayed by these previously mentioned journalistic tactics.

On Friday, April 6, 1900, John C. Wallis walked up the front stairs of the Herkimer County Courthouse in the company of another one of his mother's distant DeVoe cousins, Byron Paine. This wasn't the first time Wallis had been in the courthouse. Years ago, both he and his father had been in the civil court located on the first floor for the purpose of settling real estate matters and overdue debts. On this occasion, his divorce proceeding would be settled in the supreme court, on the second floor. When opening the ten-foot-tall double oak doors, the courtroom seemed vast. The chamber stretched from one side of the building to the other and was accented by an equally impressive horseshoe-shaped balcony. The courtroom could easily accommodate a few hundred spectators and often did, especially when there was a murder trial. This day, however, was slightly different. The *Wallis v. Wallis* divorce was on the court docket, and not one local newspaper sent a reporter to cover the proceedings. The Wallis affair was just one of several cases being read before Justice William E. Scripture.

A native of Rome, New York, the fifty-seven-year-old jurist was an 1865 graduate of Hamilton College in Clinton. Scripture passed the bar in 1867, the same year he graduated from Albany Law School. When not practicing law in the courthouses of Utica and Rome, Scripture spent every waking minute in conventions campaigning for fellow Republicans. These two pursuits served him well. In 1895, he was elected justice of the Fifth Judicial District in the State of New York by over forty thousand votes.[47]

When it came time to hear the Wallis divorce case, Judge Scripture took note that only one lawyer was present. William C. Prescott rose from his seat and informed the judge that his client and witnesses were present, but the defendant, Arvilla Wallis, was absent. After providing the judge with the legal notices from both Herkimer newspapers that proved an effort was made to locate Arvilla, Prescott called his first witness, John C. Wallis. The testimony that Wallis gave at his divorce trial was neither shocking nor new. Wallis stated where he was from, how long he had lived in Jordanville and the date he had gotten married. It was essentially the same dialogue he had with Prescott seven months earlier with two omissions. Prescott never asked about the age difference between the two when they were married, and Wallis never mentioned the fact that Arvilla had removed $1,200 from his safe when she ran away. Wallis never lost his composure and answered each question in a matter-of-fact way. When Prescott asked Wallis if his wife had ever given him a hint about where she might go, Wallis, partially perjuring himself, said, "No, sir, she never said a word; she just ran away."

When Byron Paine was called to testify, Prescott quickly moved past the "Who you are?" and "Where do you live?" line of questioning. He wanted Paine to confirm that Ben Hoyt had left the farm with Arvilla. "Well," said Paine, "he was gone about the same time and has not been seen since." Prescott then used Paine as a lead-in to introduce his star witness in the divorce case.

"Samuel Shupe lived in your neighborhood?"[48]

In the fall of 1899, Samuel A. Shupe had moved from Jordanville and had taken up residence at the Montana Boarding House on Main Street in Mohawk. As a seasonal farmhand, his services were not needed in the upcoming winter months in Jordanville. At the Montana Boarding House, he had a warm place to hang his coat, and he found steady work at a local box factory. Sometime after the first of the year, a sheriff's deputy served Shupe with a subpoena in the matter of *Wallis v. Wallis*. The fact that the two were

Court House, Herkimer, N. Y.

M13130

No one was surprised when Arvilla failed to appear at the Herkimer County Courthouse when her husband filed for a divorce. *Author's collection.*

getting a divorce did not shock him. Everyone in Jordanville suspected that something was amiss in their marriage. Besides, he had seen the legal notice in the Herkimer papers regarding the divorce proceedings. Nonetheless, Samuel A. Shupe was nervous. He feared that the secret he held so dear to his heart would soon be out in the open.

How Samuel A. Shupe came to locate himself in the Mohawk Valley is a complete mystery. Born and raised in the state of Ohio, Shupe enlisted in the navy in 1880 in Chicago and served aboard the USS *Michigan*, patrolling the Great Lakes. Discharged in 1885, he traveled to upstate New York.[49] With no apparent family ties to Herkimer County, thirty-three-year-old Samuel A. Shupe appears in the census records of 1890 as a farm laborer in Jordanville. Here, he easily found employment as a laborer but only in the spring and summer months. Shupe was so desperate for full-time work that he tried to re-enlist in the navy at the outbreak of the Spanish-American War in 1898.[50] Denied entry due to his poor eyesight, he returned to seasonal farm work in Jordanville. In the summer of 1899, Shupe discovered that his eyesight wasn't all that bad, especially when it came to Arvilla Wallis.

"Sometime in August last, were you in the house of Mr. Wallis?"

"Yes, sir," replied Shupe, adding that the exact date was August 19 and that he stayed the entire night.

"State what occurred to you when you were about to go to bed."

Shupe took a deep breath, composed himself and said, "She passed me a note that she would meet me in my room after I went to bed."

"You haven't that note with you now?"

"No, sir."

"You had a room by yourself?"

"Yes, sir."

"State what occurred."

"About midnight, she came up and got in bed with me." An impatient Prescott wanted all the particulars. "Was she in her nightclothes? What happened next?" A nervous and embarrassed Shupe tried to be as discreet as possible. "Well," he said, "she got what she was after."

Still, this wasn't enough for Prescott, who bluntly asked, "And you had intercourse with her?"

"Why, sure," replied Shupe.

Perhaps the only person in the court surprised by this candid revelation was the sitting judge. Apparently, Arvilla had no qualms about cheating on her husband with Ben Hoyt and at the same time cheating on Ben Hoyt with Samuel Shupe. The only other surprise that came out of Shupe's testimony was what transpired when he returned to the Wallis farmhouse several days after his midnight rendezvous with Arvilla. When Shupe arrived, Arvilla, without speaking a word, thrust a letter into his hand. When asked by Prescott if he still had the letter, Shupe nodded. Removing the wrinkled letter from his coat pocket, he presented it to Prescott, who announced, "I will offer the letter in evidence."[51]

As the only piece hard of evidence entered into the divorce proceedings, Arvilla's letter piqued everyone's curiosity. Thus far, all the witnesses had been men, and all the submitted statements had been made by men. While John C. Wallis called Arvilla out as an adulterer who ran away, Byron Paine provided little information other than what was needed to forge the way for Samuel Shupe to testify. Taking the witness stand, the former sailor tried in vain to protect his former lover but to no end. Although she was not present and no one appeared on her behalf to defend her, the handwritten letter was the smoking gun in the divorce. Arvilla's letter had a "bare one's soul" tone about it, coupled with a heartfelt thank-you, farewell and a touch of self pity. In her own hand, Arvilla confessed her love for Shupe, which, she claimed, was doomed from the beginning. "Had I found a friend such as you," she confessed, "it might all been different for me." Wracked with the guilt over her extramarital affairs, Arvilla wrote that she had a "horrid, wretched past" that haunted her daily. "Will God ever forgive me?" she asked while begging Shupe, "Don't waste no golden thoughts on me, for I am not worthy of it." In the most revealing part of her letter, Arvilla divulged what was missing in her married life. Trapped in a loveless marriage, without specifically naming her husband, Arvilla made it clear what had been lacking in her present relationship. "A woman craves love, affection and kindness," she said, "but how few men can see it. A kind word and a little petting goes a long way."[52]

If people from the Jordanville neighborhood attended the divorce proceedings—and no doubt some did—they didn't have time to get comfortable in their seats, as the trial was over in an instant. The court transcripts comprised only five typewritten pages. The divorce John Wallis had sought was approved on April 10, 1900.

5

DIVORCED IN DETROIT

Throughout her time in Michigan, Oretha never lost contact with her Tunnicliff cousins in Van Hornesville or her sister on the Wallis farm. Occasional letters from friends and relatives kept her abreast of the goings-on and gossip in the rural region of southern Herkimer County. No one knows for certain if Oretha was privy to her little sister's plan to leave her husband. Arvilla's appearance on her farmhouse doorstep was either expected or an eye-opening surprise. Either way, it was what Arvilla had to say that concerned her. No stranger to a failed marriage, Oretha listened intently as Arvilla described her life on the farm as Mrs. John C. Wallis.

Arvilla informed her sister that she had grown to loathe farm life and what little it offered. Nothing changed on the farm except the seasons. It was the same routine, day in and day out. While other farms in the area hired permanent domestic servants to assist with cooking and cleaning, John C., who could well afford to do so, chose not to. Maintaining two separate homes—the one she lived in and that of her widowed father-in-law—had taken its toll. She didn't want to die on the farm like her mother. As executrix of her mother's estate, Arvilla was surprised to learn that her mother didn't have a lot to show for the thirty years she lived on the Wallis farm. In addition to her clothes and a few pieces of furniture, there were five shares of capital stock in the First National Bank of Herkimer. With dividends, the stock was valued at $722.50 and had to be divided equally between David E. Wallis, her grandson John, Oretha and Arvilla.[53] What irked Arvilla was that after all those years, David E. Wallis never deeded so much as an acre of land to her mother. Arvilla took this as an omen. If John C. predeceased her, would she inherit the farm? Her instincts told her no. Because of this, Arvilla explained to her sister, she wanted a complete change in venue. She wanted to put farm life in the past and look to a future in a big city. That was her dream, and what's more, she had a man who shared this dream, Ben Hoyt. Both agreed that they would seek work and a new life in Detroit.

Oretha had her misgivings about her younger sister's future plans. The two people standing before her were not two moonstruck teenagers in love but middle-aged adults. How could they possibly exist in a city? Arvilla may have been to Utica once or twice in her life, but that paled in comparison to the thirteenth-largest city in the country. And how could Ben be of any help in this dream? On the Wallis farm, he was nothing more than a laborer earning a dollar a day working from sunup to sundown. If he was fortunate, he might be able to double his wages if he found the right kind of work that matched his meager skills. Where would they live? Once more, Arvilla had it all planned. Finding a job as a domestic servant in a wealthy household was not an option. The work she was qualified for and accustomed to was simply not an option in Detroit. Although being a live-in servant did have its advantages, with free room and board, it came with a downside. The wages were scandalously low, and the room and board were for servants only, not their boyfriends. Ben would be forced to get a job, live on his own and fend for himself. Simple economics deemed that Arvilla and Ben get jobs and live together.

All of this sounded reasonable to Oretha, but as she stared at the few trunks and belongings that made their way from the Wallis farm to her own, she still questioned how the two could afford to make their dreams in Detroit a reality. Again, Arvilla had the answer. Opening her purse, she removed a rolled-up wad of paper money totaling $1,200. Stunned at the sight of such a large amount of money, Oretha was speechless. Arvilla freely admitted to taking the money from her husband's safe before she walked out the door. She didn't consider it stealing. Instead, she reasoned that the money was due her for the many years she had worked on the farm. Oretha wasn't so sure. It was one thing to leave your husband and run away with your boyfriend, but the authorities might look dimly on absconding with a large sum of money that might not belong to you. Unmoved by the concerns of her sister, Arvilla was adamant that nothing was going to stand in her way of beginning a new life in Detroit. She assured her sister that she would contact her when she and Ben had found an apartment.

With the start of their new life in the city came new names. To their landlords (they moved twice) they were Arvilla Williams, a native New Yorker who had been married all of fifteen years to George B. Williams.[54] Assuming these aliases, the couple reasoned, served two purposes. Passing themselves off as husband and wife made it easier to rent an apartment. Although this was the last vestige of the Victorian era, societal norms dictated that you didn't share the same bed if you had different surnames. Another reason for the name change could have been Arvilla's conscience. In her mind, she may have justified taking the money from her husband's safe for "services rendered," but John C. might not agree. By this time, all of Jordanville had branded her as an adulterer. Would she be labeled a thief as well?

Detroit at the turn of the century presented as many opportunities as it did challenges to Arvilla and Ben. After securing an apartment, the couple set out in search of work. This was a totally new experience for Arvilla. Determined not to seek domestic work, she was able to obtain a factory job that paid one dollar a day, six days a week. As for Ben, the city already had an overabundance of unskilled laborers. Detroit at this time was a magnet that drew unskilled German and Polish immigrants to its burgeoning industrial centers. Ben settled for a job with an asphalt paving company. Earning about two dollars a day for six days of work, it was the first time in his life he had a permanent full-time job.[55]

For the first time in Arvilla's life, the woman who didn't have a care in the world about money suddenly had to learn how to manage a household budget. Her husband and father-in-law may have held a tight grip on the purse strings, but the taxes, both county and school, were paid on time, and there were no outstanding bills in any of the local stores. City food, she discovered, wasn't at all like food from the farm. Gone were the days of simply walking out to the barn to retrieve fresh eggs for breakfast or a chicken for dinner. There was no fresh homemade butter. You didn't have time bake bread, but you could buy a day-old loaf at the bakery. An apple orchard used for pies and cobbler was replaced by a concrete sidewalk. Semi-daily trips to the outdoor market and grocery store were not only commonplace but, like the rent, were cash transactions. In hindsight, Arvilla had to wonder if farm life wasn't all that bad. On the farm, she had a roof over her head, she never went hungry and the clothes she wore were no better or worse than what the other girls her age wore in Jordanville.

Walking a slender tightrope, balancing bills and income, it didn't bring any comfort to Arvilla that life in the big city had costly vices. One vice in particular was the availability of alcohol, something that was difficult but not impossible to secure in Jordanville. When she was a young girl, Arvilla witnessed the advent of the temperance movement, spearheaded by the Methodist church in Jordanville. "A drunken man is seldom seen here, except now and then a tramp from our sister villages," proclaimed one Jordanville resident.[56] Temperance leaders attributed Jordanville's lack of "reformed drunkards" to its lack of opportunity to obtain alcohol, as for the longest time, Jordanville never had a hotel. Those with a penchant for drinking had to travel north to the saloons that lined the Mohawk River from Frankfort to Fort Plain. Each small village had multiple taverns to choose from. While in the Mohawk Valley, Ben may have had to travel miles to get a drink, but this wasn't the case in Detroit. When Arvilla and Ben took up residence in the German neighborhood on Columbia Street, the mammoth Stroh's Brewery was just ten houses away from their front door. Added to this was the Goebel Brewery, which was situated across the street from Stroh's. The combination of these two breweries gave birth to countless neighborhood saloons scattered about the south end of Detroit. These saloons beckoned, and a thirsty Ben was only too happy to oblige.

In time, Arvilla discovered that she wasn't the only one with dreams of a new life in the city. Ben had dreams, too. However, his dream of making it big came from the bottom of a beer glass. Drunk or sober, it didn't take Ben all that long to discover that the men who frequented the local saloons were working-class men like him. His plan was to be on the opposite side of the bar, collecting the money. To Arvilla, he pitched the idea of opening his own saloon. This would not be anything like the neighborhood saloons scattered about the city but a high-class establishment. He wanted to cater to the sporting crowd and have a saloon near a ball field. The only thing he needed was money. Arvilla recoiled in absolute disbelief. Surely, he couldn't be serious. Just because you frequent a saloon doesn't necessarily mean you know the first thing about operating a drinking establishment. "He will give me no peace till he gets all the money I have in the bank," declared Arvilla in a letter to Ben's sister Rosie. "I can't go into the saloon business and one that is not decent at that. I'd rather die."[57] Granted, Arvilla stole the money from her husband, but she wasn't about to let her drunken boyfriend steal the money from her to pursue a questionable business venture.

Eventually, Ben forgot all about his dream of owning a saloon and was content to stay on the receiving end of a mahogany bar. On several occasions, Arvilla confided in her sister, she had to search around the neighborhood saloons for him. She usually found her drunken boyfriend showering his affections on a bevy of young ladies looking for free drinks. When his wages went to whiskey, her wages became strained. In time, Arvilla was forced to take money out of the bank to meet their daily living expenses. When confronted about this inequity in paying bills, Ben grew violently angry. This, too, may have put a strain on their living arrangements, as their landlady at 25 Columbia Street, Margaret Fisher, was a member of the Woman's Christian Temperance Union.[58]

Arvilla tried to be as tactful as possible when broaching the subject of Ben's behavior in letters to his sisters. When he was sober, she confided, "he treated her nicely, and she was happy, but when he had been drinking, he was an altogether different person." Another letter, this one to her sister in Yorkville, Michigan, took on a more urgent tone. To Oretha, this didn't sound at all like the jubilant sister who had visited her farmhouse several months earlier. Instead of replying to the letter, Oretha decided to see for herself. What she witnessed at the apartment confirmed her worst fears. She was greeted by a despondent Arvilla and a violently drunk Ben Hoyt. Oretha begged her sister to pack her bags and return with her to Yorkville. When she did, Ben lashed out in a drunken rage. After unleashing a storm of profanity and insults, he said he would kill Oretha if she didn't leave, and he would kill Arvilla if she didn't stay. A tearful Arvilla admitted to her sister that perhaps she had made a great mistake by throwing her life away.[59]

As she was about to leave the apartment, Oretha handed her sister an envelope from the Law Offices of Steele and Prescott. Arvilla wasn't surprised. The two-page letter informed her that her marriage was officially terminated.

> *ADJUDGED. That the marriage between the plaintiff, John C. Wallis, and the defendant, Arvilla Wallis, be dissolved and the same hereby dissolved accordingly, and the said parties are, and each of them is, freed from the obligation thereof.*
>
> *It is further adjudged that it shall be lawful for the said John C. Wallis, the plaintiff, to marry again, in the same manner as is the said Arvilla Wallis, the defendant, was actually dead; but it shall not be lawful for the said Arvilla Wallis, the defendant, to marry again until the said John C. Wallis, the plaintiff, shall be actually dead.*[60]

Included with the divorce papers was a small note addressed to her from her ex-husband. If Arvilla expected a sentimental missive along the lines of "sorry things just didn't work out between us," she was mistaken. In a polite, almost business-like way, her ex-husband inquired about what she wanted to do with her mother's personal things. Wallis wrote that he would be more than happy to sell her mother's things in Jordanville for her or ship them to Michigan. It was his way of saying that he no longer wanted any memories of her family in his house.

In Jordanville, the local press brushed aside John C. Wallis's divorce, and he hoped that his friends would do the same. Not only did he avoid the subject of his divorce in conversations with his friends, but he also did not slander or sully the image of Arvilla in public. He wanted to move on with his life. He had the farms to attend to and his aged father to look after, and he found time to strike up a friendship with one of the neighborhood women, twenty-three-year-old schoolteacher Nettie Mumford. John Wallis was content. He just wanted everyone to forget about Arvilla. And everyone did—with the exception of his aged father.

Sometime between the end of August and the first part of September 1900, a letter arrived at the Wallis farm. John C. immediately recognized the handwriting as Arvilla's. He expected the letter but was taken aback by its tone. Arvilla didn't want her mother's things at the farm sent to Michigan. Instead, she wanted to leave Michigan and return to the farm. After regaining his composure, Wallis could only surmise that she had either run out of money, or there was trouble in paradise with Ben Hoyt—or both. Wallis wasn't about to send her money, but he was curious about what had happened between Arvilla and Ben.

When the aged David E. Wallis read the letter from Arvilla, his eyes lit up and his heart raced. Regardless of what had transpired in the past, all was forgiven with the old man. He had loved Arvilla when she was a little girl, and despite the divorce, he loved her still. Unknown to John C., it was his father who had written to Arvilla begging her to come back to the farm. John C. agonized over Arvilla's request. What would the townspeople say? Running off with Ben Hoyt was scandalous, and being allowed to return to the same farmhouse she shamed defied description. He had his qualms about having Arvilla return to the farm, but his father had no misgivings. "I wanted her to come back," said the elder Wallis.[61]

In her letter, Arvilla proposed to return to the farm and take on the responsibilities as a housekeeper, just as her mother had done years before. John C. agreed to her terms and then offered his. It was important for Arvilla not to have any illusions about the arrangement. There would be no turning back the clock. Wallis told her they would not cohabitate as man and wife. She was to have her own room. He would pay her three dollars per week, which was to be paid every four weeks. Lastly, Wallis asked about

Ben Hoyt. In her next letter, in which she accepted the offer to return to the farm, Arvilla claimed she didn't know the whereabouts of Ben Hoyt. This confirmed the suspicions Wallis held that not only were the two separated, but they had run out of money—his money. A grateful Arvilla closed her letter affectionately with "love and kisses from your little girl, Villa."[62]

For the next two months, the ex-spouses corresponded intermittently. Then, toward the end of September, Arvilla wrote to her ex-husband and told him to expect her in Utica on October 4 but said she would telegraph him from Buffalo about the exact date. It came as no surprise to him that Arvilla's next letter was a plea for money to defray the cost of the trip. On October 28, Arvilla returned to the Wallis farm in much the same way she had arrived in 1868 at the age of five. She had a small trunk of clothes and was penniless.

Walking into the same house she had left eighteen months earlier, Arvilla behaved as if she had only been away for a long weekend. Not much had changed, especially in the kitchen. In her absence, the pots, pans, dishes and even the broom were in the same places they had always been. Arvilla went to work immediately, taking command of the kitchen, organizing laundry and cleaning the house. With the return of Arvilla, John C. went about his duties on the farm, knowing full well that his aged father was being well looked after. All was as if nothing had changed, he thought, with the exception of Arvilla. "She was more reserved," he said upon her return, "quieter than before."[63]

In the community, people weren't really sure what to make of Arvilla's reappearance. At the local stores and shops in Jordanville, people whispered among themselves about how strange it was that John Wallis had allowed the woman who had betrayed him back into his home. Still, there were some who believed that it had certainly taken Arvilla more courage to return than it had to leave. While many took a practical view that Wallis was thinking of the care required for his aged father, there were still others who just didn't quite know what to make of this arrangement at the Wallis farm. The press took a neutral stance: "Mrs. J.C. Wallis," reported the *Ilion Citizen*, "is again home after spending a year in Michigan."[64] In a few short weeks, the eerie silence was broken when events on the Wallis farm took a strange twist.

Four months had passed since Arvilla had returned from Michigan, and all seemed as it should be on the farm. However, on one particular occasion, Wallis arrived home from Richfield Springs at dusk and discovered a shadowy figure by the front door of his house. As he edged his buggy closer to the house, he heard a voice: "Hello there." Wallis quickly reined in his horse to a halt, for he knew that voice. It was Ben Hoyt. "Where the devil did you come from?"[65]

It was only a matter of time, reasoned Wallis, before the proverbial bad penny would show up, the only questions being when and where. While he was not exactly happy to see him, Wallis was relieved when Hoyt said he had come from Little Falls and not his hometown of Vail Mills, near Gloversville. A week earlier, it became known that a "traveling troupe of colored minstrels" had brought a case of smallpox to Gloversville. It was only after Hoyt assured him that he hadn't been exposed that Wallis allowed him in his house.[66]

Once inside, Ben Hoyt wasted no time playing the sympathy card. He couldn't find work in his hometown of Vail Mills or in Gloversville. He had no place to stay, no food and no money. With the winter months fast approaching, he was in a desperate state. Without asking Hoyt where he had gotten the money to travel from Gloversville to Little Falls and then to his farm, a gullible John Wallis offered him a place to stay for the night. Later that evening, Wallis gently pulled Arvilla aside and confronted her about Hoyt's sudden appearance on his doorstep. Arvilla claimed to be just as surprised as he was but assured her ex-husband, "He won't stay long."[67] As it turned out, he stayed the entire winter. Wallis told Hoyt he could do farm chores in exchange for his room and board with the understanding that in the spring, he would have to leave and fend for himself.

Townspeople were stunned when they discovered that Wallis was allowing the man who had broken up his marriage to step foot on his farm. Equally as shocking was that all of them were living under the same roof. The happenings at the Wallis farm were the source of gossip as well as bewilderment. The only one who could give any explanation for these goings on was John C. Wallis. He wasn't talking, and no one dared ask. People went about their business that winter while John C. Wallis counted down the days until the spring.

Although he didn't tell Ben Hoyt what to do on the farm in the way of chores, John C. nonetheless kept a watchful eye on him. So, too, did Clarence King. The thirty-one-year-old King rented the farmhouse next door to the Wallis house. As the father of four young boys, King and his wife, Mary Ann, were grateful for the work and a place to stay, but now, they were concerned that they would be evicted to make way for Ben Hoyt. "I didn't want him to do my chores," said a worried King. If Hoyt took on his farm chores, King reasoned that John Wallis would have no need for him as a laborer. King was worried to the point that he asked Wallis if he had a secure job. Wallis was

Touted as wealthy farmers by the press, the Wallis family lived modestly in this house a mile east of Jordanville. *From the* Saturday Globe.

sympathetic to his plight. He was not to worry, as he was not the problem. In a moment of candor, King said, "If it was up to me, I would make Hoyt get out." Wallis agreed. "I don't know why Hoyt won't go away and get work someplace else." After a pause, King gently broached a difficult subject. Was it because of Arvilla? Wallis shook his head. "She doesn't mean anything to me anymore," said Wallis.[68]

After the snow melted, there wasn't a day that went by that John C. Wallis didn't secretly hope that Hoyt would be absent from the farm. On April 6, his dream came true. Just before sunrise, Hoyt packed his small bag of clothes and walked off the farm without saying a word to anyone. When her ex-husband asked about Hoyt's stealth-like departure, Arvilla responded, "He didn't want the neighbors to see him, for they would say he had been kicked out." Wallis shook his head in disbelief. "Strange," he said, "when he had gone away before, he hadn't gone that way."[69] If his sarcastic implication to the way the two had left the farm in September passed by Arvilla, she simply ignored it. She assured him that Hoyt was "gone for good." Where had he heard this before? Deep in his heart, he knew he would see Hoyt again and that it was his own fault. As long as Arvilla stayed on the farm, Ben Hoyt would be a problem for him.

MAY 4, 1901

Late in the afternoon on April 6, 1901, Ben Hoyt began the long walk from the Vail Mills train depot to his boyhood home. He had absolutely nothing in the way of money to show for the winter's worth of work he had done on the Wallis farm. What little he saved while working on other farms was barely enough to pay for his train ticket home. The only thing going for Ben Hoyt was that he had a place to hang to his hat. Unlike the tension at the Wallis home, he was warmly received by his sister Gertie, whom he hadn't seen since before he went to Michigan with Arvilla. Gertie knew firsthand her brother's obsession with Arvilla Wallis. When she was working on the Ely farm, just a mile away from the Wallis farm, she frequently visited Arvilla. When her brother returned to the family home unannounced, Gertie sensed that there must have been trouble between Ben and John C. Wallis. Despite this, it didn't stop her brother from pining after his absent love. Each day, before returning home from working in a sawmill, Ben went to the post office, searching for a letter with a Jordanville postmark. Throughout April, the two exchanged letters on a fairly regular basis. Gertie, too, wrote letters to Arvilla. In one letter, she assured Arvilla that her brother was not only working but "behaving good and only drinking seldom."[70] She also begged her to please write to her brother more often. Ben constantly talked about her and missed her tremendously.

On the other hand, the content of some of Arvilla's letters worried Gertie. In one letter, Arvilla suggested that she would try to meet Ben at Fonda, as she was adamant that he should not return to the farm. "Mrs. Wallis had said," recalled Gertie of one letter to her brother, "that if [her brother] came up there again, he [Wallis] would have to walk over both their dead bodies."[71] Arvilla also made mention of the fact that her ex-husband had recently purchased a revolver. This didn't seem to bother Ben, as he declared he was "going to be prepared as well as J.C."[72] Gertie didn't understand what her brother meant by this, but she feared the worst. On or around May 2, Ben packed a small trunk of clothes and said goodbye to his sister. He told her that he was going to Gloversville to visit their brother Andrew. Gertie could only hope that her brother would be more successful in dissuading Ben from going to the Wallis farm than she had been.

Like his sister, Andrew Hoyt knew all about his older brother's infatuation with Arvilla Wallis. Going back to the Wallis farm, warned Andrew, would be asking for trouble. Despite his brother's concern for his safety, there was no reasoning with Ben. "He could not wait any longer before seeing Mrs. Wallis," Andrew later recalled. "I am going up there to see her," Ben informed his brother, "and if Wallis prevents me, he will have to walk over our dead bodies. I received a letter from her stating that she would meet me somewhere."[73] Ben told his brother that he was going to Jordanville, and he wasn't the least bit afraid of John C. Wallis. "I'm going to be sly," he said as he removed the pistol from his coat pocket, "if anything happens that I don't want to happen, but I am bound to see her."[74] Andrew let out a deep sigh. "He was sober then," said Andrew.[75] The question was whether he would be sober when he got to the Wallis farm.

From Gloversville, Ben took the train to Little Falls, and from there, he traveled to Herkimer. From Herkimer, he drank his way to Mohawk. Absolutely intoxicated, Ben stumbled about the streets of Mohawk, looking for a place to stay the night. He was most likely headed for the Montana House when he decided that this might be a good time to test his new pistol.

The gunshot was like a fire bell in the night. Excited neighbors ran outside their houses, and some went onto their porches to determine the sound's origins. Perhaps no one was more excited than Henry Voight. While walking past the National Guard Armory, Voight heard the bullet whizz by his head. The police were notified, and Chief of Police George Lovell nabbed Hoyt and brought him to the village jail. Charged with public intoxication, Hoyt was locked up for the night.[76]

Hoyt woke up the next day with a hangover and some explaining to do. Chief Lovell wanted to know what he was doing with a pistol and where he was going. Hoyt said that the pistol wasn't his—he had borrowed it from Henry Ostrander—and that he was on his way to Jordanville to return the gun and collect twenty-five dollars he claimed Ostrander owed him.[77] Incredible as it sounds, Lovell not only released Hoyt but also gave him back his pint of whiskey and the pistol—but not before collecting a fine from him for public intoxication. After paying the fine, Hoyt, having no job and no place to stay, was escorted to the edge of town like a common tramp.

Around 12:30 p.m. on May 4, John C. Wallis was chopping wood when, off in the distance, he espied a lone figure walking through a field toting a medium-sized trunk. Setting his axe aside, he went into the house. In the kitchen, Arvilla was preparing food and nursing a sore jaw. The previous day, Wallis had taken her to a dentist in Richfield Springs to have several teeth extracted. Still uncomfortable after her visit to the dentist, she listened as Wallis described the man who was crossing the fields. Arvilla shook her head and said she was sure it wasn't Ben. With that, Wallis returned to the wood pile.

Naturally suspicious of Ben Hoyt, Wallis continued to scan the horizon in between each fell of his axe. At 2:30 p.m., he returned to the house, only to discover that he had been looking in the wrong place. Seated at the kitchen table was Ben Hoyt.

"Why do you keep hanging around here?" asked an exasperated John C. Wallis.

"I have come to do business," said Hoyt.

"What kind of business?"

"That's *my* business."

"I kept you all winter," said Wallis, who was now losing his patience. "It's time you went to work. If you have any business to do, I want you to do it and get out."

"I'll do my business when *I* get ready."[78]

Tension and tempers escalated quickly, and this was quickly followed by name calling and profanity. An emotional Hoyt, having fortified himself with a pint of liquid courage earlier that day, insisted that he would not leave without Arvilla. John Wallis, finding it impossible to argue with a drunk, demanded that Hoyt leave his premises. At the height of the verbal encounter, old David Wallis, having returned home from visiting a neighbor, entered the kitchen and seated himself in the corner while Arvilla openly sobbed. In this chaos, barbs and insults went back and forth for almost an hour. A compromise between the three was out of the question. Someone had to yield. The question was: Who would it be?

THE NEW SHERIFF

I n December 1887, the Herkimer County Board of Supervisors, precursor to the present-day legislature, received a disparaging report from the New York State Prison Commission. Not only was the county jail "25 years behind the times," the commission stated, but it was "inadequate to accommodate the class of people it was built to shelter" as well. The report shouldn't have surprised anyone. For generations, the board had miserly maintained the facility. Since the jail's completion in 1834, the board moved tax dollars to more worthwhile projects, such as the construction of roads and bridges. The jail was never deemed a high-priority project to the local politicians. It was, after all, a jail, not a five-star hotel. Some argued that if prisoners had complaints about the living conditions in the jail, they should look into a better line of work and stay out of jail.

The commission's report simply highlighted the obvious. The interior of the jail itself hadn't changed since the first prisoners were brought there in 1834. Its dungeon-like interior was out of step with the changing times. Women, children and those who were identified as less dangerous personages were still housed in the poorly ventilated, windowless attic in lathe and plaster rooms. The other prisoners experienced worse conditions. Straw tick mattresses on the floor or placed on planked sawhorses were their lot. As many as three individuals could be crammed into the three-foot-by-nine-foot limestone cells, while the larger cells could accommodate up to a dozen men. Sanitation conditions all the way around were crude. Not only did each cell have its own slop bucket, but quite often, prisoners also went to trial wearing the same clothes they had been wearing when they were arrested.

The report concluded with a terse directive: either build a new jail or remodel the present one. The board of supervisors met and weighed their two options. If they constructed a new jail, there was the question of its location. The present jail was directly across the street from the county courthouse and thus made the transfer of prisoners to and from county court more practical. If a new jail was constructed, it would most likely have to be built on the outskirts of the village of Herkimer or in another township. In the end, the deciding factor was the price tag. When the board learned that a new jail would cost the taxpayers over $100,000, they opted to renovate the present jail.[79]

Renovations began in the first week of February 1898 and continued into the summer months. While prisoners tried to make themselves comfortable in their new accommodations in the horse stables, manual laborers went to work dismantling the limestone interior brick by brick. When the wood-plank floors and beams were removed, the workers installed twelve-inch-thick I beams to support the concrete floors. All the cells had steel walls, and the doors were made of either solid steel, with a rectangular opening to receive meals, or had the traditional vertical bar look. The attic was unnecessary and, as such, was sealed off for good. A separate hallway on the second floor was reserved for women and children. Perhaps the greatest innovation could be found in the sanitation facilities. Not only was there indoor plumbing on each floor, but also a shower was installed for the men on the second floor, and the women's and children's wing had a clawfoot bathtub. All vestiges of the old jail had been removed. When Dan Strobel became sheriff in January 1901, he walked into a virtually new jail.

What he lacked in a formal education (he quit school at the age of twelve) Strobel gained from his hard work and determination. Born on his father's farm in the village of Cold Brook on October 26, 1860, Daniel F. Strobel entered the field of local politics in a time when he couldn't even cast a vote for himself, as he was eighteen years old. When he wasn't farming, felling trees, operating his own lumber company or dabbling in business opportunities in Utica, he was involved in county politics. Strobel first expressed an interest in running for the office of sheriff in 1894 but was unable to garner enough support at the Herkimer County Republican Convention. In those preprimary days, delegates put candidates on the November ballot. Undeterred, Strobel tried again three years later. On this occasion, he was successful in getting on the November ballot but failed to win the general election. Joseph Baker defeated him by 789 votes.[80] Three years later, Strobel was once again on the November ballot. On this occasion, Strobel campaigned vigorously, enlisting support from every township. His tireless efforts did not go unnoticed by the local press. On the eve of the election, the *Ilion Citizen* confidently predicted that "D.F. Strobel will be elected by a handsome majority." This prediction came true, as Strobel won the race by 896 votes.[81]

The new sheriff was no different than any of his predecessors. Strobel viewed the office of sheriff as the largest political plum Herkimer County had to offer. No one who wore the sheriff's star considered it a capstone to their political career. For many, it was just the beginning. The county had a long history of ex-sheriffs who went on to bigger and better things. Some were elected to the state assembly or sought political appointments in Albany, and a few tried to get to Congress.

In addition to being a political plum, the sheriff was also handed a golden apple. This was the highest-paying elected position a nonmember of the bar could hope to achieve in the county. The annual salary of $7,560 included free room and board at the jail. Although the jail had taken on a whole new look with its renovations, the spacious living quarters Strobel and his wife, Carrie, would occupy for the next three years were antiquated but comfortable. The sheriff regularly supplemented this income by collecting civil fees, serving summons and making arrests. In his first year as sheriff, Dan Strobel banked $8,906.75.[82] Since a sheriff could serve only one term, many of them set money aside in their political "war chests" for their future political endeavors. A consummate politician, Strobel never let his eye stray too far from the political horizon. He was, as one Utica reporter observed, one "who plays politics 365 days of the year."[83]

When Strobel took over the reins of the sheriff's office on New Year's Day 1901, he took on an administrative position. His chief responsibility was to maintain the jail. In his first few months as sheriff, his jail population included a forger, an army deserter, several petty thieves and a few charged with assault. What angered Strobel the most was the number of tramps, hobos, nomads or "Weary Willies" who occupied the jail. These individuals often committed petty crimes for the purpose of having a warm place to stay and hot meals during the winter months. Having them stay in their cells at the expense of the county taxpayers didn't sit well with Sheriff Strobel. A broad-shouldered man with deep-set eyes and a Teutonic mustache as thick as a paintbrush, Strobel believed able-bodied men should work as he had. In his youth, he supported himself by felling trees in the Adirondacks. Not only did he believe that these Weary Willies needed to be put to work, but he had an idea of how to do it. If the state prisons were putting prisoners to work, reasoned Strobel, the county should, too.

In March, he submitted a written report to the board of supervisors that caught everyone off-guard. Strobel proposed that inmates of the county jail be put to work repairing the village streets and county roads. His plan was quite simple. Boulders from the surrounding farms would be brought to a lot next to the jail where a sledgehammer-wielding gang of prisoners could crush them into small stones to be used on the county roads. The county, reasoned Strobel, got much-needed crushed stone, and the Weary Willies earned their keep at the jail.[84] Well aware that saving the taxpayers money always looked good on one's political résumé, the local press applauded his efforts to save the county money. The board of supervisors, however, rejected the idea.

As April led to May, the jail was running smoothly. The spring-like weather was mild, and it seemed like the perfect weekend to get away. Strobel went downstairs to the booking area and was in the process of telling a few of his deputies of his vacation plans when the phone rang. A deputy picked up the receiver and then motioned toward Strobel. The caller was a highly excited individual who said he could talk to only the sheriff. When Strobel took the phone, the caller identified himself as Clarence King of Jordanville. Deputies nearby saw the look of calm on the sheriff's face suddenly turn to that of concern. King informed the sheriff that there had been a shooting at the Wallis farm and that two people were dead. Momentarily stunned by this news, Strobel regained his composure and pressed the caller for more details. King claimed that was all he knew, as he wasn't present when the shooting took place. He did say that his employer, John C. Wallis, had shot a man and then directed him to contact the sheriff.

After receiving directions to the Wallis farm from King, Strobel directed his undersheriff, Erwin E. Kelley, to bring the automobile around to the front of the jail. While Kelley saw to this, Strobel placed a series of telephone calls. The first was to District Attorney George W. Ward in Dolgeville, and it was followed by calls to the coroner's office and lastly to photographer Albert Zintsmaster in Herkimer. Almost as an afterthought, Strobel went upstairs and told his wife that their planned vacation would have to wait.

It took two hours for Strobel and Kelley to traverse the unlit country roads in southern Herkimer County to reach Jordanville. For the two lawmen, locating the Wallis place was relatively easy, as buggies and automobiles lined both sides of the road near the farm. After parking their automobile, the two walked by a small crowd and made their way up the walkway that led to the front door. As the front door was open, Strobel and Kelley walked in unannounced and went directly to the kitchen. Of the dozen or so men in the kitchen, one stepped forward, extended his hand and introduced himself as John C. Wallis. "I suppose you have come for me."

Taken aback by Wallis's congenial welcome, Strobel was momentarily speechless. "That is all right," said Wallis reassuringly. "There lies my dead wife, shot by Ben Hoyt, and there lies Hoyt, shot by me."

Strobel couldn't believe his eyes or his ears. Did Wallis confess? In the corner near the woodshed door was the slumped-over body of a man, and in the middle of the kitchen floor was a Victorian-era fainting couch. Lying prone on the couch was the body of a woman whose arms had been folded across her chest. Casually walking over to the kitchen table, Wallis picked up a pistol and presented it to Strobel. "Here is the revolver I used," he said.[85] When asked where the other murder weapon was, Wallis said he hadn't bothered to look for it but was sure it had to be near the body of Hoyt. After surrendering the weapon, Wallis briefly described to the sheriff what had happened.

Wallis gave a thumbnail sketch of his wife and hired man running off to Michigan, his divorce and her eventual return to his house in the role of a housekeeper and caregiver to his father. When Hoyt left his employ in April, Wallis said he had thought that was the last he would see of him. But sometime between 1:00 and 2:00 p.m. that day, he saw Hoyt crossing one of the distant fields.

"I went in," said Wallis, "and told my wife that Hoyt had come back. She acted nervous and pretended to be afraid. She said Hoyt would kill her. Shortly after Hoyt came in the kitchen, I told him to go away and get work elsewhere; it being spring, he could easily find work. He promised to go once and then he said he wouldn't."

For the next several hours, the two argued back and forth. Finally, according to Wallis, Arvilla had her fill.

It was understood between her and myself that in case Hoyt came back, she was to go away to get rid of him. I left the kitchen and went to my room to get a newspaper which contained the railroad timetable. My father was in the kitchen with them. I was delayed in finding the newspaper. Before I got it, I heard two shots and screams from my wife. Seizing a revolver which lay on top of the safe in my room, I rushed back to the kitchen. As I approached, my wife said, "He shot me." Hoyt was moving toward the door. He flourished the revolver at me. Then he changed it from his right to his left hand tried to open the door. As he did so, he fired at me, and I opened fire on him, shooting three times, after which, he fell to the floor. I went at once to the assistance of my wife. I held her in my arms and asked, "Villa, don't you know me?" She motioned as if she did and, shortly after, expired in my arms. I then laid her on the sofa.[86]

Wallis concluded his soliloquy by stating that what he did was completely justified. It was quite simple: Hoyt killed Arvilla; he then shot at Wallis, who killed him in self-defense. Strobel then said that self-defense or justifiable homicide wasn't for him to decide. But someone who would have a lot to say on the matter was presently walking into the house. His name was George W. Ward.

The thirty-one-year-old district attorney walked into the kitchen and carefully surveyed the murder scene. In the year and four months Ward had been district attorney, he had never investigated a murder. Looking back at the small crowd that had followed him into the house, he motioned to Albert Zintsmaster to come forward while, at the same time, he told everyone else to stand back. One of the premier portrait photographers in Herkimer, Zintsmaster set up his tripod and camera in such a way as to effectively capture the murdered victims on a glass-plate negative. He adjusted the lens of the camera and, holding steady a tray of magnesium powder mixed with potassium chloride, pressed an electric charger. A blinding flash lit up the room. For the next picture, Zintsmaster found it necessary to prop up the body of Ben Hoyt by closing the woodshed door. After this picture was taken, he packed up his equipment. Any other pictures the district attorney required could wait until the morning.

While Zintsmaster packed up his equipment, Ward turned his attention to Ben Hoyt. Kneeling down next to the body, he adjusted his left leg. Clutched in his left hand was the pistol. After prying the pistol from the hand of Hoyt, Ward recognized it as a .32-caliber, five-shot revolver with four spent shell casings. If Arvilla had been shot twice, as John Wallis claimed, where were the other bullets? Wallis told the district attorney the same story he had told the sheriff earlier that evening. Ben Hoyt shot at him first, and he returned fire. An examination of the kitchen wall where Wallis claimed he stood when he shot at Hoyt revealed no bullet holes.

Things got worse for John C. Wallis before they got better. When going through the pockets of Hoyt's jacket, Ward discovered a half-empty bottle of whiskey. In another pocket were several letters. The letter from Michigan addressed to Rosie Hoyt in Gloversville didn't hold much interest for him; however, a small handwritten note did, as its contents were foreboding: "This

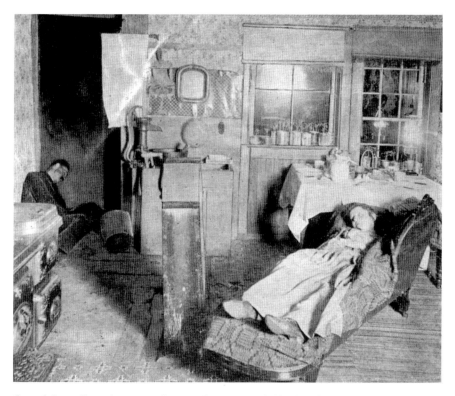

One of the earliest crime scene photographs was recorded in the Wallis kitchen by Zintsmaster. *From the* Saturday Globe.

is to certify that if I meet with any trouble, I give my clothes to my brother and my trunk and any other paraphernalia to my sister Gertie. Ben Hoyt."[87]

The missing bullets, together with the apparent suicide note, reinforced Ward's belief that something was amiss. From the moment he walked into the kitchen, he knew that things weren't right. The body of Arvilla lying prostrate on a fainting couch looked like a centerpiece in a macabre play. Her face had been wiped clean of bloodstains, and her arms had been neatly folded across her chest to hide the bullet wounds. Added to this, the floor had been mopped clean of blood. The fact that Wallis admitted that he couldn't be sure what time the shooting took place made it more suspicious. Too much time had elapsed between the shooting and the phone call to suit the district attorney. The same thing had happened seventeen years earlier on the Druse farm. Roxalana Druse had plenty of time to rearrange her kitchen after decapitating her husband and pulverizing his body into bits with an axe before incinerating the remains. Roxalana did her best to hide

Although Wallis did embrace his ex-wife before he was led to jail, he probably wasn't wearing a full-length fur coat in early May. *From the* Saturday Globe.

the evidence, and as far as George W. Ward was concerned, so did John C. Wallis. Turning to Town Justice Windsor Maxfield, Ward instructed him to fill out the papers charging John C. Wallis with murder in the first degree, and in the same breath, he ordered Strobel to take him to jail.

Wallis, who had remained stoically calm up to this point, suddenly got excited. Going to jail wasn't what he expected, and he vehemently protested. Not only was this a case of self-defense, but he couldn't go to jail, as he had to make arrangements for Arvilla's funeral. "After that," said Wallis to Strobel, "I will come to Herkimer of my own free will."[88] The sheriff gently pulled the distraught Wallis aside and told him that under the circumstances, he might want to cooperate. Besides, said Strobel, any funeral arrangements he wished to make could be forwarded to the undertakers from the jail.

Before Wallis was escorted out of the kitchen, he walked over to the body of his former wife. Lifting her into his arms, he embraced her and kissed her several times. "She was my wife," he said, "and I always loved her, ever since she was five years old, when I first saw her. I loved her now. And when she eloped with Hoyt and asked to be allowed to return here because she feared him, I was glad to take care of her. I felt that I was bound to protect her." It was, as one newspaper recalled, "a pathetic farewell…a spectacle which brought tears to the eyes of all present."[89] Ward didn't know what to make of the performance. Was this staged for his benefit, or was this a genuine expression of grief?

8

THE PRESS AND JOHN C. WALLIS

Prior to the murders, few people outside the township of Warren had ever heard the name Wallis; they were also unaware of the peculiar living arrangements on the farm. When news of the double homicide with its love triangle twist swept through the county, the public clamored for the gossipy details. Over the years, newspaper editors had come to monetarily appreciate stories of this nature. H.P. Witherstine was living proof of this. The former editor of the *Herkimer Democrat* made a small fortune reporting on the Druse murder in Warren and reaped even bigger rewards when he issued a special "execution" edition of his paper covering the hanging of axe murderess Roxalana Druse on February 28, 1887.

Reporters didn't have to do a lot of deep research when writing about the murder of Arvilla Wallis and her paramour. All they had to do was go to the first floor of the Herkimer County Jail and interview John C. Wallis. In the past, Roxalana Druse was cautioned by her attorney to not give interviews to the press, but John C. Wallis, on the other hand, just wouldn't shut up. When reporters from Utica, Herkimer and Little Falls descended on the jail, Wallis seemed eager to tell his side of the story. The only question was whether Wallis granted these interviews with the blessing of his attorney.

Wallis retained the same legal service he had used for his divorce. Although Amos Prescott acted as his divorce attorney, his present dilemma was placed in the able hands of Abram Steele. The former district attorney who sent Roxalana Druse to the gallows knew all too well the power of the press in formulating public opinion. Before the first person was sworn in to

Herkimer County Jail.   Herkimer, N. Y.

Brought to the Herkimer County Jail on the evening of May 4, John C. Wallis occupied a cell on the first floor. *Author's collection.*

testify in the Druse trial, the press had already condemned Roxalana. She never elicited any sympathy from the press for her heinous crime. Steele now hoped the exact opposite would happen for Wallis. Unfortunately for attorney and client, the first press release was damaging.

George W. Ward hadn't even left the Wallis farmhouse when someone made it to the nearest telegraph office with news of the double homicide. The following day, May 5, the Sunday edition of the *New York Herald* ran a story that infuriated Abram Steele. The headline "JEALOUS OF DIVORCED WIFE, HE SLEW HER" informed readers that John C. Wallis "killed to-night his divorced wife, aged forty, and her hired man, Benjamin Hoyt, aged thirty-five. Wallis has been living apart from his wife since last November. This evening he went to her farmhouse and shot her when she responded to his knock. He then shot and killed Hoyt through jealousy."[90] In an article littered with errors, the *New York Herald* absolved itself of irresponsible reporting in a manner befitting the press. Instead of accepting the blame in the next issue, it simply told readers that through the diligent investigating of Sheriff Strobel, the affair had "quite a different story."[91] Regardless of the rebuttal, Abram Steele was concerned. More than a few people in Jordanville believed that John C. Wallis had shot Arvilla and Ben. "If he did all the shooting," reported the *Gloversville Daily Leader*, "it might be difficult to convince a jury that he was not justified."[92] It was a sentiment shared by Abram Steele.

As it turned out, John C. Wallis inadvertently initiated his own public relations campaign. While lying on his cot in jail, he reiterated many of the details of the murder he had previously made at his farmhouse in the presence of the sheriff and district attorney. One reporter observed that, "in all, he gave about a dozen versions of the tragedy."[93] The press described Wallis as a well-to-do, hardworking farmer, respected by all who knew him. Everyone sympathized with his failed marriage and, at the same time, uttered their absolute amazement at what eventually transpired. "Now comes the strange part," is how the *Herkimer Democrat* led into the story of Wallis letting his ex-wife return to his house and later allowing Ben Hoyt to live there for the winter months.[94] One reporter quipped that Wallis was to be, in a way, admired. "[His] patience in tolerating the liaison between the loafer Hoyt and his wife was indeed a virtue."[95]

When portions of Wallis's jailhouse interview were printed in the local press, Abram Steele could not have been more pleased. There was, as one paper called, "a unanimity of sentiment favorable to Wallis."[96] Another paper echoed this view and mentioned a topic that Abram Steele believed needed to be addressed. "Sentiment in the town of Warren is strongly with Wallis," recorded the *West Winfield Star*. "His neighbors accept his story that he acted in self-defense and scoff at the idea he did all the shooting. And even if he did, there are many who would justify such action."[97]

In all of his interviews, Wallis never spoke disparagingly of his former wife, even after she ran off with Ben Hoyt; nor did he speak ill of her when she came cowering back to the home she had abandoned. His comments regarding Ben Hoyt were equally crafted. He had his own opinions regarding Hoyt, and he let the press have theirs. In this, the fifth estate was absolutely ruthless. When one reporter canvassed the Jordanville neighborhood, he discovered a universal disdain of Hoyt. "They say Hoyt should have been shot ten years ago."[98] Perhaps the mildest comment regarding his character came from the *Little Falls Evening Times*: "Hoyt was regarded as a fairly good looking fellow," declared the *Times*, "with nothing but his looks to commend him to respectable people."[99] Later, the editors of the *Times* had a different opinion of him: "Hoyt has not a single friend in the neighborhood. He was a lazy, good for nothing loafer who was ugly and quarrelsome when in his cups [drinking] and treacherous and cowardly when out of them."[100]

On the eve of the coroner's inquest, a few editors and pundits had their say in the press. No one denied that what had happened on the Wallis farm was a terrible tragedy, but many agreed that it could have been prevented. "A little love is a dangerous thing," reminded one editor, "when it is given in forbidden directions. One husband is all that any woman may safely have at one time. It is best to be off with the old love before you are on with the new."[101] In Dolgeville, one resident couldn't help combining moral depravity with the possibility of a costly murder trial. "If every man would stick to his own, instead of some other fellow's wife, what a world of trouble and expense it would save."[102] Still, the *Freeman's Journal* in Cooperstown perhaps said it best: "Don't Make Love to Another Man's Wife."[103]

THE CORONER'S INQUEST

When the Herkimer County coroner arrived at the Wallis farmhouse on the night of the murder, the first person he greeted was, in all likelihood, his brother, the sheriff. Dr. Charles G. Strobel didn't attend the school of hard knocks like his brother. Instead, he chose the academic path. After attending Fairfield Seminary and Cazenovia Seminary, Strobel enrolled in Long Island Medical College, where he graduated in 1888. Upon his return to Herkimer County, the twenty-four-year-old established a medical practice in Dolgeville.[104]

At the Wallis residence, Dr. Strobel conferred with fellow townsman George W. Ward regarding the time and place of a coroner's inquest. It didn't take Dr. Strobel long to discover that Jordanville didn't have much to choose from in the form of places that could comfortably seat a large crowd. It was his hope to avoid the problems that had taken place the last time an inquest occurred in Warren. The choice of Eckler's cheese house for the Druse inquest proved to be woefully inadequate. Neighbors and associates of Roxalana Druse crammed themselves into the tiny cheese house, and the overflow crowd had to stand outside in the January snow. The following day, the inquest was moved to a hotel in Little Lakes. Although Dr. Strobel didn't have to contend with the weather, he felt certain that the Hoyt-Wallis inquests would attract, like the Druse inquest, a standing-room-only crowd.

While conferring with Justice Maxfield about when and where the inquest would take place, Dr. Edward H. Douglass and Dr. Allison O. Douglas began the grisly task of performing an autopsy on the body of Arvilla. After

Dr. Charles G. Strobel received compliments from the community as well as the press for the way he conducted the inquest. *From the* Saturday Globe.

lifting her body from the fainting couch, the doctors placed it on the kitchen table. Cutting away her bloodstained blouse, the doctors discovered several letters tucked into the folds of her corset. These were passed on to Dr. Strobel, who, in turn, gave them to the district attorney. Ward thought this odd as he glanced at the postmarked letters. Why would Arvilla have letters she had written to Ben Hoyt on her person? Shouldn't these letters have been discovered in the coat pockets of Ben Hoyt?

As the kitchen was poorly lit, the doctors ushered Clarence King to come forward with his kerosene lantern. As he held it high above the corpse, the doctors began to cut away at the flesh and probe for the projectiles. As blood flowed off the table and settled into large pools on the kitchen floor, Martha King stood by outside the kitchen. The wife of Clarence King had the unenviable task of mopping the kitchen floor.[105]

By morning, news of the double homicide had spread quickly throughout the valley. When David Wallis arrived home after spending the night at a neighbor's house, he discovered that a large group of sightseers had descended on his property. By midafternoon, an estimated five hundred people had arrived at the Wallis farm. A few were neighbors, but most were strangers who had traveled for several miles to see for themselves the scene of the crime. The eighty-four-year-old took it all in stride, mingling inconspicuously with the crowd. To his great delight, a few of these amateur detectives took the time to explain to him what happened. Pulling one such person aside, Wallis pointed and said sarcastically, "There's a fellow over there who knows more about it than you or I do." It was only after Wallis walked up onto his porch and was ready to enter his house did the crowd discover who he really was. "Have a good time, boys," he said.[106]

That same afternoon, Dr. Strobel received the autopsy report. Having read it, he sent a copy to the district attorney and saw no reason to not release a copy to the press.

In the case of the woman, it was found that one bullet entered about 3½ inches below the right breast and one inch from the medial line [the middle of her body], *passing through the liver and lodging in the spinal marrow. The second bullet penetrated three inches above the same breast and, in a transverse line, [passed] through the right lobe of the lung and [lodged] in the back. In the case of the man's autopsy revealed that one bullet entered his head near the left temple, second, the upper part of his right arm and the third the right hand.*[107]

Included with the report were the bullets extracted from the bodies. These were sent to George W. Ward, as the district attorney was in possession of the murder weapon. As Ward discovered, the paragraph-long report left more questions than answers. There was no question that the wound to the temple of Ben Hoyt had been fatal. But if he was shot in the temple, it would indicate that he was not facing John C. Wallis. As for the two bullets taken from the torso of Arvilla, neither doctor ventured a guess about the trajectory of either of them. Was she shot as she looked at her assailant face to face, or was she shot from an angle? Apparently, Dr. Strobel must have been satisfied with the report, as he immediately released the bodies to the undertakers.

As in many rural communities, there was only one undertaking establishment. In Jordanville, it was Wayman and Hyde. These undertakers assured John C. Wallis that the burial of his former wife would not take place until they had received a telegram from her sister in Michigan. Meanwhile, any other arrangements he desired to make would be fulfilled. The night before the burial, Wallis was, according to witnesses, inconsolable. He ate little and slept less that evening. "He begged fervently," observed a reporter, to be allowed to attend the funeral but was denied by Sheriff Strobel, who "could not take responsibility of allowing a man charged with a capital offense to go on such an errand."[108]

At 2:00 p.m. on Tuesday, May 7, a carriage arrived at the Wallis farmhouse. A woman dressed in black stepped down from the carriage and slowly made her way to the front door. Entering without knocking, she made her way into the first room on the left. Oretha Crane walked toward the wooden casket to say goodbye to her sister. Her escort for this solemn occasion was her son John, who, a year earlier, had been employed on the Wallis farm. After a few prayers offered by Reverend Cross of the Methodist church, the undertakers placed the casket in a horse-drawn hearse for the mile-long journey to the cemetery. At the graveside, there were more mourners and more prayers. One hundred yards away, there were neither. Andrew, Edward and William Hoyt stood by as grave diggers lowered an $18.50 pine box containing the remains of their brother into an unmarked grave.[109]

John C. Wallis testified that he never touched the body of Ben Hoyt. Zintsmaster adjusted the body slightly for this image. *From the* Saturday Globe.

Meanwhile, back in Herkimer, Abram Steele paid an unannounced visit to the county jail. Having been informed that the day of the inquest had been set for May 9 at Wayman's Hall in Jordanville, Steele wanted to prepare John Wallis for what to expect. First, Steele tried to set Wallis at ease. A coroner's inquest was not a trial. Its purpose was to gather information to establish the cause of death that occurred under questionable or suspicious circumstances. No one could make any formal accusations or allegations at the inquest. In short, its purpose was to gather information, not to lay blame. Nonetheless, Steele told Wallis that, once more, he would have to tell the story of the shooting. Although Justice Maxfield would preside over the inquest, it would be Coroner Strobel who would direct questions to any of a number of people who had contact with either his former wife or Ben Hoyt. When the coroner was satisfied with the testimony the witnesses had given, he would step aside and allow the defense attorney and the district attorney to do the same.

For his defense counsel, Wallis relied on the talented ex–district attorney Abram Steele. *From the* Saturday Globe.

As for Abram Steele, the ex–district attorney who had successfully convicted Roxalana Druse of murder in 1885, most everyone in Warren knew of him. Few of the farmers in that region knew of George Ward. A native of Illinois, Ward had moved east with his family when he was a young boy, eventually settling on a farm in Fort Plain in Montgomery County. After attending a rural school, Ward enrolled in Clinton Liberal Institute. In 1883, he graduated from Columbia Law. After a brief stint as a newspaper reporter for the *Kansas City Star*, Ward relocated to Dolgeville and opened his own law practice.[110]

Steele cautioned his client not to be intimidated by George Ward. At the turn of the century, Herkimer County housed a stable of good lawyers, and Ward was considered by his contemporaries as one of the best. Short in stature but strong in ambition, the current district attorney was not to be underestimated by any means. He had an aggressive style of examining witnesses in the courtroom that was tantamount to bullying. This was clearly evident on May 23, 1896, in Little Falls City Court when Ward represented a farmer who was sued due to wages denied. When the plaintiff's wife, seventy-year-old Martha Cole, took the witness stand, Ward grilled her mercilessly. The old woman was so unnerved that she rose from the witness chair and threw herself to her knees in the middle of the courtroom and prayed out loud for all the lawyers in general and George Ward in particular. She finished her prayer and retained her seat, and Ward went at her again. Mrs. Cole left the witness chair and went to her knees a second time, asking "God to check the attorney in his way and show him how to follow in His footsteps and keep in His path of righteousness and kindness."[111]

10

A FORCED MARRIAGE?

Unlike a trial, a coroner's inquest did not necessarily follow a rigid schedule. Quite often, the coroner would consult with the attorneys to determine whether their scheduled court dates were in conflict with the date chosen for the inquest. In the instance of the Hoyt-Wallis inquest, not only did several days elapse between sessions, but several venues were chosen to accommodate attorneys, coroners and witnesses as well. When Coroner Strobel called the first session on Thursday, May 9, the second session wasn't called until Tuesday, May 14. In the interim, the press took it upon themselves to keep the public informed of the latest news, editorials or, in some instances, gossip.

While reporting news of the inquest to the public was entrusted to reporters, quite often interpreting what happened at the inquest fell upon the newspapers' editors. In Ilion, the man who shared his own thoughts on the Hoyt-Wallis affair was the multitalented Rufus E. King. A native of Potsdam, New York, where he graduated from normal school at the age of seventeen, King furthered his education with a liberal arts degree from Syracuse, and he eventually became an ordained Methodist Episcopal minister. After serving his flock for twenty years, King set his robe aside and, at the behest of friends, became the editor of the *Ilion Citizen*. Writing under the nom de plume "The Man About Town," King offered his insights on a variety of subjects, including the fate of John C. Wallis.[112]

Echoing the sentiments of many people, King wasn't totally convinced that John Wallis was innocent. "To be sure," he wrote, "there was some speculation immediately after the shooting as to whether Wallis was not guilty of shooting both his divorced wife and Ben Hoyt." When David E. Wallis took the witness stand as an eyewitness to the murder, King expressed his cautionary approach when interpreting the events of the murder. "Blood" he wrote, "was thicker than water, and if Wallis did shoot the woman and the man, the father would naturally shield the son."[113] Despite this apprehension, King nonetheless expressed his admiration of the defendant. "Mr. Wallis evidently thought a great deal of the woman, else he would not have allowed her to live under his roof again after she eloped with Hoyt." While others heaped a great deal of criticism on Wallis for doing this, "The Man About Town" took the opposite stance. "None can deny that he proved himself a kind and generous man. If Wallis had the disposition of some men—most men, I may say—he would have spurned the woman who left him for another."[114]

In nearby St. Johnsville, fifty-nine-year-old W. Irving Walter was keenly interested in the double homicide. Unlike the educated "Man About Town," the "Sage of St. Johnsville" possessed a one-room schoolhouse education. However, what Walter lacked in higher education, he made up for in his natural command of the English language. A frequent contributor to all the newspapers in Utica and the Mohawk Valley, Walter could be counted on to express his views on presidential candidates, the Spanish-American War and local history. On the subject of the Jordanville murders, Walter had plenty to say. With the murder of William Druse at the hands of his axe-wielding wife Roxalana in 1884 still fresh in the minds of the public, Walter said that this was the tip of the iceberg. "The town of Warren," he wrote, "has been the theater of many regrettable occurrences."[115]

Unlike Rufus King, Walter reminded his readers that blood wasn't always thicker than water. This was especially true when it came to the Dykeman family. On the night of November 1, 1873, a highly intoxicated Ben Dykeman arrived home and discovered that his cousin Alfred Travers was in his home. Dykeman accused Travers of having improper relations with his wife, who just happened to be home at the time, and she, too, was fairly intoxicated. In the scuffle that ensued, Travers proceeded to pound Dykeman senseless with a cast-iron teakettle. For good measure, he stabbed him as he lay unconscious on the kitchen floor. Travers pleaded self-defense, but the jury didn't believe him, and the judge sentenced him to life in prison at Auburn.[116]

In some instances, reported Walter, it wasn't a case of "blood is thicker than water" so much as it was simply a case of bad blood. "A long and bitter quarrel had existed between the house of Edick and the house of Shaul," was the report from the *Little Falls Journal and Courier.* Although related by marriage, the Shaul and the Edick families were Warren's equivalent of the Hatfields and McCoys. Their longstanding feud reached a boiling point on the evening of November 19, 1870. Apparently, Sebastion "Boss" Shaul thought it was time to pay the Edicks a visit. With the elder Edick away from the farm, Mrs. Edick summoned her next-door neighbor Henry Fort to her home for protection. While in the Edick house, Fort caught sight of Boss Shaul peering into a window. Fort immediately made his way to the front porch to investigate. Upon opening the front door, Fort came face to face with Sebastian's son Menzo. No one knows for sure if words were exchanged, but we do know Menzo Shaul shot Fort in the groin. The following day, with father and son in jail, a "party of roughs made a raid upon their house, broke windows, and frightened an old lady and an unmarried daughter, behaving in a very disorderly and improper manner." Fort recovered and successfully sued, and the Shaul-Edick feud continued.[117]

If you didn't have an axe, a gun or even a teakettle, you can always go the route of Nancy Lyman. On December 8, 1869, she went on trial for the arsenic poisoning of her second husband. When her first husband of twenty or so years died, Nancy married fifty-eight-year-old Ephraim Gardner on January 18, 1868. Several days later, the new Mrs. Gardner purchased, among other things, arsenic at Bell's Store in Jordanville. She claimed to have a problem with rats at the farmhouse, but that was nothing compared to her husband's soon-to-be stomach problems. Ephraim Gardner died on March 10, 1869. The grieving widow settled the estate in three days, and on April 27, she married for a third time. Her third husband was seventy-four-year-old Frederick Lyman. The sudden way Ephraim Gardner died, coupled with the timing of Nancy's next marriage, raised eyebrows in the close-knit neighborhood of Jordanville. Enough townspeople cried foul play that the body of Ephraim Gardner was exhumed. On April 1, his stomach, bowels and a small portion of his liver were sent to Albany for analysis. When traces of arsenic were discovered, the body was re-exhumed six days later. As expected, heavier traces of arsenic were discovered in his liver.[118]

Awaiting her day in court, Nancy Lyman expressed her complete dismay at being in the Herkimer County Jail instead of being on her honeymoon. According to her, this was a simple misunderstanding. Taking the witness stand in her own defense, she did not deny purchasing the arsenic, mixing it in a bottle and pouring it on the rat traps scattered about the house. Placing the bottle on a kitchen shelf, Nancy Lyman told the court that her husband must have mistaken the arsenic bottle for a liquor bottle. When she was declared not guilty, one juror came forward and admitted that he was not totally convinced of her guilt. A great many people in the town of Warren may have disagreed.[119]

Nevertheless, all of the stories W. Irving Walter related were in the past. This was, after all, a new century, and the Hoyt-Wallis murder was the topic of conversation throughout the county. As the public eagerly awaited the next issue of the local newspapers to read the latest happenings surrounding the inquest, John C. Wallis was perfectly satisfied with the way all the valley papers had reported the events of that fateful afternoon. Unfortunately for him, on the first day of the inquest, May 9, the *Little Falls Evening Times* published an article that completely unnerved him. Under the headline "Married Against Her Will," the *Times* claimed that the marriage between Arvilla and John C. had been doomed from the beginning. Arvilla was a young vivacious girl who wanted her own life, but she was "compelled by her parents to marry Wallis." It was no wonder that she once tried to elope with the Casler boy on the next farm.

With public opinion leaning in favor of Wallis, the *Times* article painted him in a different light. At the time of his marriage, Wallis was, according to the paper, "a miserable old bachelor…given little to society." It was not a match made in heaven as much as it was a match made at the bank. The marriage was founded on how much financial security he could provide. "He had MONEY," reported the *Times*, "that god whose fetish worship has brought so much misery into the world." True love, happiness and contentment, added the *Times* are "not commodities listed on Wall [Street]." Of their childless union, the paper asserted, "Wallis knew enough to make money, and nature taught him how to make love, though it is said that he was an inept student."[120]

For this startling exposé, the *Little Falls Evening Times* relied on information provided by an anonymous source, a woman. "I was not surprised when I heard of the murders," she said, "I have expected such result for the past year. But I cannot think of the dead woman as the one that was the most to blame." Then living in Utica, this woman claimed she was not only a classmate of Arvilla but also a close confidant. "Her enforced marriage," she claimed, "ruined her life." Time and again, she claimed Arvilla sobbed when the subject of marriage between her and her stepbrother was discussed. To her friend, she confided "a thousand times she had rather die than marry him, and sometimes, she threatened suicide." The marriage, she claimed, was rocky right from the start and didn't soften with age. "Of course, she

Zintsmaster took this picture of a weary John C. Wallis in the county jail. *From the Saturday Globe.*

was unhappy," said Arvilla's classmate, "she was a slave to the family and became a common drudge. She liked society and some pleasure, but she was held to the farm and its round of drudgery and never went anywhere."[121]

Eventually, this source claimed, Arvilla could no longer endure her existence on the farm. "She ran away with Hoyt to punish her husband. He had been particularly nagging and mean to her for some time, and she left with the hired man in a fit of anger. It has been said that she took some of her husband's money when she went, but it is my opinion that she took only what she had a right to." Lastly, still echoing the theme of money, this anonymous source argued that the only reason Arvilla was asked to return to the farm by her former husband was because it saved him the "expense and trouble of finding someone to take care of the old man [David Wallis]."[122]

Many people believed that the letter would have been far more convincing had the author identified herself. There was a broad brush line between fact and parlor room gossip. In Jordanville, local townsmen rallied and stood by one of their own. Wallis, they said, "loved his wife, and they lived happily together until the hired man had caused trouble between them."[123] Residents of Jordanville were inclined to ignore this latest missive. The one person who did not ignore the story was sitting in the county jail.

When the usually reticent John C. Wallis read the story of the forced marriage, he flew into a rage. Desperate to protect his image, Wallis was anxious to refute everything that had been published about him in the article. "It is not so," he told a reporter from the *Times*. "I never heard an intimation of such a thing until now. There was no hesitation on her part. She was entirely agreeable to our marriage. We were engaged for two years, and when the ceremony took place, she was twenty-one and I was thirty-five." Engaged for two years? When Arvilla hosted her party in Jordanville on the evening of March 20, 1884, there was no mention of her fiancé being in attendance. As they were married on September 24 that same year, they were, at most, engaged for six months.

As for Arvilla's unsuccessful carriage escape with the Casler boy, Wallis fumed. "This article says my father stopped her from eloping before our marriage. It is very strange that he never told me about it, and I never heard about it from anyone until now." Stranger yet was the fact that during the inquest, the elder Wallis was never asked to substantiate this story.

Wallis claimed that he and his wife had their disagreements, but by and large, theirs was a happy marriage. "We lived happily together," said Wallis, being quick to mention that in all of Arvilla's letters in the possession of the district attorney, not one insinuated that he had been unkind to her.

"I never took her anywhere," scoffed Wallis. This, he claimed, was a blatant lie. "She went with me on many trips, and I would have been glad to take her on many more, but she seldom wanted to go."[124] Here, Wallis perhaps lied. Jordanville may have lacked a local newspaper, but it didn't lack local correspondents who submitted their one- or two-line vignettes to the valley papers. The *Ilion Citizen*, *Herkimer Democrat* and *Richfield Springs Mercury* had columns for all the crossroad communities and hamlets in southern Herkimer County. A birth, an illness, an accident, church news and visitors did not escape these local correspondents. In their fifteen years of marriage, John C. Wallis never took Arvilla to Michigan to visit her sister. If and when they left the farm, it was only to go to Jordanville or Richfield Springs. If Wallis had taken his wife anywhere, it would have been recorded in the Jordanville column of the newspapers. She may have visited her Tunnicliff cousins in Van Hornesville, but other than that, Arvilla never went anywhere.

When the *Times* reporter raised the question about the money Arvilla allegedly took from his safe when she left the farm, Wallis acted indifferent. Arvilla, he said, always had money. In addition to receiving the profits from the sale of butter and eggs, Wallis said, "I always gave her money when she asked for it." If this was true, said the reporter, then why did she feel it necessary to take $1,200 from the safe when she fled with her paramour to Michigan? Here, Wallis chose his words carefully: "I never said she did." Addressing the "drudgery" aspect of life on the farm, Wallis expressed complete bewilderment. "She never acted as though she thought her position was that of a drudge."[125] On this point, Wallis might have chosen his words more carefully. Her position may have implied to the public that Arvilla was a hired housekeeper instead of his wife.

Wallis desperately wanted to refute the most damning quote from the *Times* piece. "She did not run away with Hoyt to punish me," he said. Without ever giving his opinion about why she ran off with Hoyt, Wallis, instead, changed the subject to why she returned to the farm. "She said I had always been good to her." When pressed by the *Times* reporter if it was a mistake to take her back as a housekeeper, Wallis replied, "We could have got others to do the housework for what we agreed to pay her, but we could have got nobody that would have fitted in our family so well." In hindsight, Wallis said that the only mistake he ever made was allowing Hoyt to return to the farm. "I can see that very plainly now."[126]

Finally, Wallis reminded the reporter of what he had said on numerous occasions: he and Arvilla were terrified of Ben Hoyt. "He was a desperate man," said Wallis. The only reason Wallis tolerated Hoyt was to avoid trouble, per Arvilla's wishes. When asked what his plans after the inquest were, Wallis told the reporter they would largely depend on whether he was acquitted. Providing the charges against him were dropped by the district attorney, Wallis, in a philosophical moment, said, "I would like to get away and forget what has happened here, but my father wants me to stay on the farm, and it is my duty to stay with him. I shall probably take a trip somewhere to recuperate and occupy my mind with thoughts of other things." Would that trip be to California?

Early in the week, George Ward went to the jail and presented Wallis with two letters that had been addressed to him and kept in the care of the district attorney's office. The letters were from Mrs. Mary Perkins and Mrs. Mary Myers. The two were widows with money and no children, and they asked him to visit California at their expense. After reading the letters, Wallis shook his head in disbelief. "Those widows out in California who wrote me? Well, I guess I won't bother myself about them that much. This is a strange world, and the people in it do strange things."[127]

11

"MY OWN DEAR BOY"

For the small town of Jordanville, the Hoyt-Wallis inquest was about as close to live entertainment as anyone could get, complete with an all-star cast, supporting ensemble and standing-room-only crowd. Like the star of a gala premier, John C. Wallis was immediately besieged with well-wishers upon his return to Jordanville. Here, Strobel felt no need to place handcuffs on Wallis and allowed him wander aimlessly through the crowd, where he was warmly received. He shook hands with many of his friends, exchanged pleasantries and was reunited with his father, who he hadn't seen since the shooting. After a short while, Strobel nodded to Wallis and motioned him to Wayman's Hall. Justice Maxwell, who was to preside over the inquest, had just arrived with Coroner Strobel.

The proceedings were not yet underway when a local citizen approached George W. Ward and presented him with a petition signed by 158 residents of the township. "We respectfully ask you to fully exonerate John C. Wallis upon this investigation, as we believe he not only acted in self-defense but vindicated the sacredness of our American homes, and the outcome will be a warning to the immoral and evil disposed."[128] Unmoved by the contents of the petition and its endorsements, Ward handed the document to Abram Steele without comment. A jury of his peers, not the signatures of his friends, would determine the fate of John C. Wallis. In order for Ward to achieve that end, he needed more facts regarding the dual homicide than opinions offered by the local newspaper editors.

The first witness called by Coroner Strobel was, not surprisingly, his own brother. When Dan Strobel related the details of his arrival at the Wallis farm in the early evening hours of May 4, he not only distinctly recalled the amiability and cooperative nature of John C. Wallis, but more importantly, he gave a detailed description of the kitchen as well. With Arvilla's body on the fainting couch in the middle of the kitchen and that of Ben Hoyt slumped over by the woodshed door, the crime scene looked too neat. Everything was in order, and there was not a speck of blood anywhere.

Sheriff Daniel F. Strobel never forgot how calm and cooperative Wallis was when describing the murders. *From the Saturday Globe.*

The only other law enforcement official to testify was Village of Mohawk police chief George Lovell. His testimony was a bit shocking, because hardly anyone at the inquest knew that Hoyt had spent the night before the murder behind bars. Lovell described how Hoyt had been arrested in his village for discharging a firearm within the village limits while publicly intoxicated. When Lovell testified that he had released Hoyt and returned his pistol and whiskey to him, it stunned the inquest's audience. He was immediately chastised by the local press. "If the Mohawk officials who had him in custody Saturday morning had sent Hoyt to the penitentiary for two or three months, his passions might have cooled, the woman's infatuation might have subsided."[129]

After Chief Lovells's testimony, a parade of about one dozen witnesses who either lived in the village of Jordanville or resided close to the Wallis farm came forward. Orchestrated by Abram Steele, these witnesses were not so much character witnesses as they were character assassination witnesses. From Willard Yule, who recalled how Hoyt once broke into his house, to Clarence King, who accused Hoyt of arson, it seemed that everyone had nothing good to say about the deceased. Henry Ostrander, on the other hand, took his opportunity on the witness stand to correct the testimony that Chief Lovell had previously given regarding the ownership of Hoyt's pistol and the money Ostrander owed Hoyt. Ostrander was adamant on the subject. He most certainly did not loan Hoyt a revolver, and what's more, he didn't owe him any money. "On the contrary," said Ostrander, "he owes *me* money."[130]

Those in attendance paid close attention to the testimony and came to an early conclusion that everyone had a story to tell, and quite often, they contradicted someone else's story. When Oretha Crane was called to testify, she presented, as one newspaper claimed, "the most sensational evidence of the day."[131] Arvilla's older sister came to the inquest with a dual mindset. She was determined to solidify the martyred image of her sister within the community and, at the same time, damn Arvilla's former lover for all eternity. The train ride from Michigan to the Mohawk Valley gave her plenty of time to rehearse her lines for her presentation at the inquest.

First and foremost, Oretha wanted to clear up a popular Jordanville misconception of her sister happily "eloping" with Ben Hoyt. "She said she went away with Hoyt," claimed Oretha, "because he compelled her to, for she was afraid he would harm her."[132] Oretha certainly got everyone's attention with her opening statement. Heads turned at the inquest as the audience clamored for more details about the relationship between Ben and Arvilla. As for their husband and wife charade in Detroit, Oretha did everything she could to describe it as a living hell for her sister. "She was in mortal fear of him," she said.[133] On the subject of alcohol, Hoyt, she claimed, was half drunk half of the time and totally drunk the rest of the time. All of his earnings were spent on whiskey while Arvilla struggled to pay the rent. "He had been ready to desert her," said Oretha, "and just hung around hoping she would have some money."[134] Hoyt was a violent drunk, and as their relationship grew more volatile, Oretha feared for her sister's safety. "I went to Detroit," said Oretha, "and *I* persuaded her to leave Hoyt and return to Warren."[135] Those closest to John C. Wallis found this hard to believe. The consensus among the neighbors was that Arvilla returned to the farm at the behest of the elder Wallis.

At the conclusion of her testimony, Oretha Crane rose from her seat and, in a strong voice, made a most incredible statement: "I am intensely interested in having the man punished who murdered my sister," she announced. "I think that man was Benjamin Hoyt."[136] Exactly what she had in mind for punishment for a man who was presently lying in an unmarked grave was not clear.

When Oretha Crane testified, she backed up her claims that her sister lived in fear of Ben Hoyt while they were living in Detroit by reading passages from Arvilla's letters. What made her testimony more compelling was that the next witness, her daughter-in-law, did essentially the same thing. Ella Brown of Burlington Flatts in Otsego County brought with her two letters written to her by Arvilla after her return from Michigan. In a letter dated March 14, 1901, Arvilla wrote, "I am awfully unhappy. Ben Hoyt is hanging around here, and we cannot get rid of him. My God, how I have suffered for my folly in going away with him. If he would only leave me alone, I would have some comfort in life, for John C. is very kind to me." A month

MRS. JOHN C. WALLIS.
[From what is probably her latest photograph.]

Arvilla Tunnicliff Wallis in what is believed to be her last photograph. *From the* Saturday Globe.

later, a much relieved Arvilla confessed, "I thank God Ben Hoyt has gone out at last, and I think John C. and I are going to move up on the other place and run the farm. I hope I am rid of Hoyt for good, and if he ever comes back, I will be over to your house in a hurry. He will think I have gone to my sister's home in Michigan."[137]

The information contained in these correspondences, together with the testimony provided by Oretha Crane and Ella Brown, proved to be in direct contrast to the testimony given by the Hoyt family. The shy nineteen-year-old Gertie Hoyt said that she was the intermediary in the Hoyt-Wallis relationship. As her brother was semi-illiterate, it was she who not only wrote his letters to Arvilla but also read her letters aloud to him. When George W. Ward presented her with a few correspondences addressed to "Mrs. Arvilla Wallis," Gertie pointed out that it was indeed her handwriting. "I wrote some letters for him to Mrs. Wallis," said Gertie, "once or twice a week—at his direction."[138] Of the several letters her brother left behind at Vail Mills, Gertie read aloud passages written by Arvilla to her "Babe," showering him with kisses and affection. In one particular letter, dated April 28, Arvilla suggested that for his own safety, Ben should not return to Jordanville, as John C. had recently purchased a revolver. Instead, Arvilla suggested that they meet in Fonda. Setting the letter aside, Gertie told the inquest audience that this was what prompted her brother to purchase his own revolver.

When Andrew Hoyt testified, the twenty-seven-year-old took the opportunity to refute what Oretha Crane said about Arvilla's return to the Wallis farm. "When Ben came from the west," recalled Andrew, "he came to Gloversville. He said John C. had written Mrs. Wallis a letter, wanting her to return. He said Ben was to stay home a couple weeks and then go to Wallis. When he returned in April, he said Wallis hadn't used him very well." When asked by George Ward if he was acquainted with Mrs. Wallis, Andrew replied with perhaps too much candor. He said that he, too, served as a hired man on the Wallis farm alongside his brother Ben, and as such, he was acquainted with Mrs. Wallis. "I was sent for by Mrs. Wallis; she wanted to see me," recalled Andrew on one occasion. "I was in Wallis's parlor one night after midnight. Mrs. Wallis was attired in her nightdress."[139] At that point, a startled Ward told Andrew Hoyt that no further information had to be divulged.

While Oretha Crane, Ella Brown and Gertie Hoyt read snippets of Arvilla's correspondences, the press featured one letter in its entirety. It was one of the letters the doctors performing her autopsy had discovered in her corset, and it somehow made its way into every newspaper from Utica to Gloversville.

[Saturday]

My Own Dear Boy,

It seems that I cannot stand it. That I must write to you every day, it's all the comfort I have now. Oh, "Ben," it makes me feel so lonesome I can hardly stand it. When I read your letters over where you ask me if I had gone back on you and was going to give you up? No, babe I am never going to give you up as long as I have breath of life. Every beat of my heart is for you. If you knew how I was grieving for you, you would never doubt me or my love again. Just the minute I close my eyes I see you and all the places when we were happy and when I do sleep, and that is not much, I always dream that we are so happy, and you are so good to me. I cry until I can't cry no more and tired out then I drop to sleep only to awake to find a world of sorrow and grief. Last night it just seemed to me that you did not get my letter and had ventured up in the barn.

I went out on the stoop and looked over so many times and just at dusk imagined I saw something white up in that square hole, so I called "Pete, come Pete" and just then Len Snyder came to see about painting the house so when they [John C. and Snyder] got talking I went and put up the parlor window and I kept going in after J.C. went to bed after 12 o'clock, but no Ben did I see, so gave up and went to bed, but not to sleep, only to cry and worry about my babe.

Now, Dearest, I am going to try and get away Monday or Tuesday, but he says I will have to be a G—d— sight sharper than we were before if I ever get away with you. He watches my every move. This morning after [Clarence] King went into the field I made an excuse that I would go down and see where the hens were sitting. So I went in the barn thinking you might have stayed there. I called, "Babe, Babe," twice and went out and when he was coming down that way. I said, "You must be afraid I will get lost." Oh, I was so mad. In a few minutes he went down, and I pretended looking all around for hens. He was gone quite a while.

He is sawing up some limbs today. He has cleaned the yard and keeps an eye on the house worse than ever since he saw that last letter. Oh, Ben! It just makes me feel like killing myself over coming back here. I don't believe I could ever live over the last four weeks. I would not, for dear, the longer you are gone the harder it is for me to keep up. All that I can do is just look at my babe's picture and think till it seems I would go wild. If I don't get where you are soon, I believe I will go crazy. My heart beats so fast that it makes me sick. I have cried myself just about to death. Oh, why does God put this love in our hearts if one has to be parted like this. I will either send a telegraph or letter just as soon as I get to Richfield [Springs] so that you can get to Fonda the same as I do. Now, dearest, I will send this so it will go out tonight if I can see Louise Ostrander go up. She goes up almost every Sunday. Then you will get it Monday morning. I will go Monday or Tuesday sure, Goodbye my loved one.[140]

From the tone of this letter, it certainly did not appear that Arvilla was living in fear of Ben Hoyt as Oretha Crane and Ella Brown were led to believe. Aside from the affectionate overtones of the letter, many of Arvilla's claims and accusations came under the scrutiny of the inquest officials, as well as the general public who read the letter. It was difficult for any of the neighboring farmers to believe that John C. Wallis watched her every move. A man who ran two farms and had hired men to look after and direct hardly had the time to shadow his former wife.

Arvilla's assertion that John C. said that she and Ben "would have to be a G—d— sight sharper" the next time they left the farm is debatable if not comical. When she ran away from the farm with her paramour in September 1899, it was a swift, clean break. Their late afternoon buggy ride to Little Falls gave them ample time to board a westbound train. John C. Wallis may have had an inkling about where they were going, but nonetheless, the two lovebirds had a twelve-hour head start.

Her promise to meet Ben Hoyt on either Monday, May 6, or Tuesday, May 7, should have been addressed at the inquest. When George W. Ward arrived at the farmhouse on the evening of May 4, he made note of the fact that Arvilla's trunk was packed. Clearly, she was going to leave the farm, but where would she go? Didn't it seem odd that neither John C. nor his father asked her earlier that day why her trunk was packed?

Lastly, her claim that John C. was watching her "worse than ever since he saw that last letter" sounds suspicious. Would Arvilla be so careless as to leave a letter out in the open for all to see and perhaps read? If she had, it was a cunning move on her part, as it served two purposes. She hoped it would either make John C. jealous or make Ben Hoyt more desperate to resume their relationship. When Ben arrived at the farmhouse that Saturday, Arvilla must have known that there would be a confrontation between him and her ex-husband. If Ben shot and killed John C., the former would go to state prison while she would remain on the farm and continue to care for the old man. When he died, there was the possibility that she would be named the executrix of the estate, and as such, she would inherit a small fortune. If John C. killed Ben Hoyt in self-defense, life on the farm would remain the same. She would continue her caregiver duties, and there was a slight chance that she and her ex-husband could reconcile. In all of these possibilities, the only thing Arvilla didn't count on was the possibility that she might get herself killed.

12

THE WALLIS MEN TELL THEIR STORIES

The next two witnesses were the only eyewitnesses to the murders, and everyone at the inquest was eager to hear what each of them had to say. Regardless of the fact that the story of the murder had been told and retold in all the valley papers, the sitting audience wanted to hear firsthand what had happened from the lips of those who were present. To this end, they were not disappointed.

The reporters from the Utica newspapers were most impressed with David E. Wallis. He was not the curmudgeonly old man they had expected. "The elder Wallis," observed a reporter from the *Utica Observer*, "is in some respects a remarkable old man. Although past the four-score year mark, he is hardy and appears to be in excellent health."[141]

In his own folksy way, the octogenarian told of his early life in Warren and how, as a recent widower, he came to employ Jane Tunnicliff as a housekeeper, who, years later, became his second wife. Of his son's marriage, Wallis maintained that it was fine until Ben Hoyt came into the picture. When Ben and Arvilla went to Michigan, Wallis said that he moved back to the house to live with his son. He told the inquest audience that he was pleased with the return of Arvilla but terribly disappointed with the return of Hoyt. As the town was rife with gossip when this occurred, David E. Wallis now had a chance to comment on their living arrangements. "John and Arvilla did not live together as man and wife," he explained, "she slept in the hall bedroom. Hoyt, when he was here, slept in the room above."[142]

According to the elder Wallis, he had just arrived home around 2:00 p.m., after having an early dinner at the home of Byron Paine. Walking into the kitchen, he was surprised to see Ben Hoyt sitting at the table and became concerned when he noticed that Arvilla was sobbing. While Wallis was confused about what was happening, events became clearer when Arvilla shouted, "You are drunk, and there is no use talking to you!" At this precise moment, John C. walked into the kitchen. "That's what you are always telling John," said Hoyt. Arvilla was quick to respond. "You go off and get drunk and spend all your money in bad places and then come back here."[143]

Most everyone agreed that it was David E. Wallis who encouraged Arvilla to return to the farm. *From the* Saturday Globe.

Naturally, Hoyt denied this and quickly changed the subject to marriage. "You know," said Hoyt, "you promised to marry me on the first of May." According to David Wallis, his son and Arvilla were stunned at this piece of news. While John C. questioned this, Arvilla denounced it. "That's a lie," she said emphatically. When Hoyt said he had the letters to prove it, the elder Wallis tried to call his bluff. "If you have the letters," he said, "why don't you show them."[144] Unbuttoning his coat, Hoyt reached into his pocket, produced several letters written by Arvilla and threw them on the kitchen table.

Unnerved at the sight of the letters, Arvilla rose from her chair and exclaimed, "I ain't going to stay here with this damned set any longer! I am going out to Michigan to get away from you all! You can all go to the devil!"[145] She stormed out of the kitchen and went upstairs, leaving Hoyt face to face with John C. Wallis. "Ben," said his former employer, "it is time you went to work like a man. I have kept you all winter. You came here in a peculiar manner. You didn't ask to make any arrangements." Before Wallis was able to complete his lecture on self-discipline, Arvilla reappeared. She turned toward her stepfather and declared, "I want you to pay me what you owe me."[146]

David E. Wallis recalled that he was taken off guard by this statement, as he was already aware that his son had paid her seventy-two dollars for her services in April.

"What do I owe you?" he asked. Arvilla reminded her stepfather of her dowry. "You promised when I was sixteen years old that if I would stay and help, you would pay me $500 and that if I married, I should have sufficient to go housekeeping. Have you done it?"

"No, but I'll see to it. I haven't the money now." She then turned to her former husband and said, "Will you take me to the train?"[147]

According to testimony given by David E. Wallis, as soon as his son left the kitchen to retrieve the train schedule in the adjacent room, events quickened. Wallis illustrated how Hoyt removed his pistol and approached the victim. Brandishing his revolver, Wallis recalled a frightened Arvilla exclaimed, "Oh, he is going to shoot me!"[148] At this moment, Coroner Strobel asked if he could demonstrate how the shooting took place. The coroner seated himself, taking the place of Arvilla, and Wallis would act the part of Ben Hoyt. In a rare moment of levity, David E. Wallis, using a pencil as the barrel of the pistol, leaned forward and, in an aside, told the coroner that he would not shoot him too hard. As Wallis approached the seated coroner, he recalled how Hoyt grasped the seated Arvilla by the breast with one hand and aimed the revolver within inches of the other. After receiving two shots to the torso, the grievously wounded Arvilla tumbled out of her chair and onto the floor. It was only at this moment that David E. Wallis said his son reentered the kitchen.

Hoyt, claimed the elder Wallis, was unsuccessful in his escape from the kitchen, due to the latch on the woodshed door being stuck. "Give it to him, John," he shouted, "he shot Villa!" After the shooting ceased, David E. Wallis said he and his son rushed to the side of Arvilla. As his son cradled her in his arms, he pleaded, "Villa, don't you know me?" The elder Wallis tried to feel for a pulse as Arvilla drew her last breath. Turning toward Hoyt, David E. Wallis asked his son if he was dead. "I don't know," he recalled his son saying, "but he ought to be."[149]

The testimony presented to the inquest by David E. Wallis raised just as many questions as it provided answers for George W. Ward. First, could the letters that were found in the folds of Arvilla's corset during the autopsy be the same letters that Hoyt tossed on the kitchen table? If so, did she hide the letters herself before she was shot, or did John Wallis do it after she was murdered? Then there was the question of money. How ironic was it that when Ward searched the pockets of Ben Hoyt that there was exactly seventy-two dollars in one pocket? Did Arvilla give Hoyt her wages earlier, or did John C. Wallis plant the money on him? What exactly did Arvilla say to make Hoyt become so desperate? More important than this was the question of who shot who first. Was it possible that after shooting Arvilla, Hoyt, horrified that he had killed the woman he loved, paused long enough for John C. Wallis to shoot him in the left temple? Using the utmost care in questioning the affable old gentleman, Ward asked who fired first: Hoyt or his son? "The truth of the matter is," replied David Wallis, "this tragedy has unstrung me. I am spoiled."[150] In other words, the old man wasn't quite sure who shot at who. At this juncture, Ward took a cue from Rufus "The Man About Town" King, who, in his recent editorial in the *Ilion Citizen*, cautioned everyone about family protecting family. If Arvilla, asked Ward, was indeed murdered by John C. Wallis, would David, as John's father, testify against him? "I certainly would!" bellowed the old man in a voice that boomed across the hall.[151]

At the start of the inquest, District Attorney George W. Ward was not totally convinced that John C. Wallis was innocent. *From the* Saturday Globe.

The next witness to be sworn was the only other eyewitness to the murders. "The star witness in the examination of John C. Wallis," declared a reporter from the *Little Falls Evening Times*, "was Mr. Wallis himself. He made a strong witness on his own behalf and testified to nothing which will change the popular sentiment in his favor."[152]

Recalling the petition that was presented to him earlier, asking for Wallis to be "fully exonerated," Ward knew that there was only one way to turn public opinion away from the defendant. It had to come from the lips of John C. Wallis. If Wallis erred, misspoke or retracted a statement, George W. Ward might have a chance of convincing the inquest that this homicide was not justifiable and should go to court. Ward listened intently for over an hour as Wallis recalled the timeline leading up to the shootings. During this soliloquy, Wallis took the liberty of dispelling a few rumors surrounding the circumstances of his former wife's return to the farm. Earlier, Oretha Crane had testified that her sister, as she recalled, "wanted to be on an equal footing with him and his father as to the property." Wallis cleared up this misconception immediately. His former wife, he told the inquest, was to assume the duties of housekeeper and healthcare provider for his father. As for the passage in the letter Arvilla had sent to Ella Brown regarding them moving up to and running another farm, Wallis was adamant on the subject. There was to be no "equal footing" as far as the property was concerned, and there was to be no reconciliation. The divorce was final. He vaguely hinted that he had plans for his own future, and Arvilla certainly wasn't a part of them.

Wallis didn't briefly explain the events that led to the shooting. In fact, he recited the events as if they had occurred the previous day. Giving careful attention to detail, he not only set the stage and placed the characters in their positions in the kitchen, but he provided the entire dialogue as well. While looking for the train schedule in the *Richfield Springs Mercury* in the room adjacent to the kitchen, Wallis said he heard Arvilla scream followed by two shots.

"I grabbed my revolver and ran to the kitchen," said Wallis. "As I caught sight of Villa, she exclaimed, 'He's shot me!' and blood gushed from her mouth. I kept moving ahead and saw Hoyt with a revolver in his hand, and if my eyes and ears did not deceive me, he pointed it at me and fired." Wallis said he saw the muzzle flash from Hoyt's gun and momentarily hesitated. "I caught hold of the hammer of my revolver; it didn't work. Then I realized that it was self-acting, and I got it going. I shot at him three times."[153]

George W. Ward was immediately suspicious of this testimony. He had no problem with the history of the firearm. Wallis said he had bought the revolver about a year earlier at Peckham's Hardware and Plumbing Goods Store in Richfield Springs, being careful to add that it wasn't purchased for the purpose of dealing with the likes of Ben Hoyt. An inspection of the store accounts could easily verify this claim. What was difficult to believe was that Wallis, since the time of the purchase, claimed to have fired the pistol at least twenty times. To Ward, it was difficult to accept that Wallis, after being shot at by Hoyt, fumbled with this pistol and still managed to get off three shots at a moving target. Furthermore, what were the odds of having a loaded revolver in the same room he entered to retrieve the train schedule?

"Why did you come out of the room with that revolver?" asked Ward. "You were not in any danger in there, were you?"

"I wanted to see what Hoyt was doing," replied Wallis.

"Didn't you know he would be punished if he shot anybody and that you didn't need to shoot?"

"I don't know if I thought of that."

"Are you sure Hoyt shot at you?"

"Yes, sir. I maintain that he did."

"Are you sure?"

"Well, I may be mistaken, but my belief is that he did."

"Did you think at the time that he shot at you?"

"I did."

A *Saturday Globe* artist relied on the testimony of John C. Wallis to reconstruct the shooting. *From the* Saturday Globe.

"If you were afraid of Hoyt, why didn't you have your revolver in your pocket?"

"I am not in the habit of carrying it."

"Didn't you think you might have occasion to use it when he came back?"

"I thought I could reason with him, as I had been kind to him all winter. I grabbed the revolver to defend myself."[154]

Wallis's quick responses to these questions didn't surprise anyone at the inquest. After all, in almost every interview with the local press Wallis staunchly stood by his story. This was a case of a man protecting himself in his own home. To drive this point further home, Abram Steele asked if there was a possibility that, in the melee, he could have shot Arvilla.

"I say on my oath," proclaimed Wallis, "that I fired at nobody but Hoyt and that none of the shots from my revolver struck Arvilla." It was the shots from Hoyt's revolver that concerned George W. Ward. Of the four empty shell casings in Hoyt's revolver, Ward could account for three. Chief Lovell accounted for one of them when he testified that Hoyt had discharged his weapon in Mohawk, and the autopsy of Arvilla accounted for two more.

While Wallis claimed that Hoyt fired at him first, no evidence of a bullet hole in the kitchen wall was ever discovered. Was it possible that Wallis killed Hoyt in cold blood and then took the revolver and fired it outdoors to make his claim that Hoyt shot first plausible?

When Steele asked if his client considered himself a good shot, Wallis's response was self-deprecating. "I don't know," said Wallis, "I have shot a revolver a good many times."[155] No one knows if any of Wallis's fellow townsmen in the audience snickered or rolled their eyes. John C. Wallis was an avid hunter who had grown up with guns his entire life. His nearby neighbor Alma Shoemaker remembered him as a "crack" shot, and eight-year-old Howard King called Wallis a "dead shot" after witnessing him "place a nickel in a beehive and shoot at it." Drunk or sober, Ben Hoyt was no equal to John C. Wallis in a shoot-out.[156]

13

THE MUTE WITNESSES

I n 1853 in Southampton, England, Henry Goddard was called to the residence of a Mrs. Maxwell to investigate a burglary. Goddard, a member of the Bow Street Runners, the first organized police force in London, arrived at the scene and interviewed the only eyewitness to the event, Joseph Randall, the house butler. Randall claimed that he was awakened when a burglar entered his room and shot at him while he was in bed. "Here," said Randall, "is where the bullet struck the bedboard." Randall said he immediately shot at the burglar, who then fled the scene.

Goddard wasn't about to take this story at face value. He removed a penknife from his pocket and gently lifted the bullet from the headboard. In a classic case of "the butler did it," Goddard compared the bullet (it had a distinct raised mark on it) to the bullet mold in the possession of Randall. It was an exact match. For the first time in recorded police work, Goddard had traced a bullet to its gun. Caught in an obvious lie, Randall made a full confession. By "foiling" an attempted break-in, he had hoped to receive "a reward from his mistress for his bravery in protecting her property." The butler didn't receive any compensation from Mrs. Maxwell, but he did receive a sharp rebuke from the local magistrate.[157]

Forty-eight years later and an ocean away, George W. Ward wanted to do the same thing. Before the inquest was underway, Ward delivered the two murder weapons and the bullets recovered from both bodies to officials at Remington Arms in Ilion. Ward and Steele were also aware of the fact that there were a great many people who, days into the inquest, continued to believe that John C. Wallis was responsible for both deaths. The *Johnstown Daily Republican* was one such publication that voiced this opinion. "Wallis, it is true, had abundant motives to kill both his wife and her paramour and who thought he had ample justification....Was it possible that Hoyt's shots failed to take effect, while those of Wallis did, and that he killed his wife as well as Hoyt?"[158] The only way to either dispel these rumors or justify these claims was to have these key pieces of evidence examined by professionals at Remington Arms. The extracted bullets from the deceased were, as Rufus E. King referred to in his latest editorial, "mute witnesses" to the murder.[159] Their silence was broken on the last day of the inquest.

When Hazen W. Bradley was sworn in to testify, he introduced himself as the superintendent of Remington Arms. "I have been engaged in the manufacture of firearms for twenty-six years. I am experienced in the rifling of firearms."[160] After a careful examination of the pistol used by Ben Hoyt, Bradley came to the conclusion that the .32-caliber handgun had a distinct left twist to the rifling in its barrel. The bullets recovered from the body of Arvilla Wallis exhibited a left twist as well. To prove his point, Bradley displayed a cast of the barrel and placed it by one of the bullets. The left-hand twist was an exact match to that on the bullet.

Melvin Hepburn, the superintendent of the gun department at Remington Arms, came to the same conclusion. Conducting his own analysis of the weapons, Hepburn testified that the bullet removed from the leg of Ben Hoyt exhibited a right-hand twist, the same right-hand twist that was found in the rifling of the handgun used by John C. Wallis. "The bullets found in the body of Mrs. Wallis," said Hepburn, "couldn't have been fired from [the Wallis] revolver."[161]

Two experts in the firearms industry conducting two different tests and both reaching the same conclusion was great news to Abram Steele and his client. What further proof was needed? This proved what John C. Wallis had said all along. Hoyt shot and killed Arvilla, and he shot and killed Hoyt in self-defense. Ward, satisfied with the information provided by these two expert witnesses, announced that he had no further questions to ask. That being said, Coroner Strobel closed the proceedings.

It isn't known if those in attendance left the inquest in an orderly fashion, but it is fair to say that several dashed away. These people would have been reporters who were attempting to get to their newspaper offices as quickly as possible to submit their stories for the next edition. All agreed that the ballistic evidence supplied by officials from Remington Arms guaranteed that John C. Wallis would soon be a free man. Not wishing to rush judgment, the conservative editor of the *Little Falls Evening Times*, John Crowley, remained optimistic and expressed his faith in Coroner Strobel. "The coroner," said Crowley, "is a clear-headed, sensible man, and he may be depended upon to render a verdict that will be in accord with all the facts and public sentiment." Given the existing evidence and testimony presented at the inquest, Crowley was thoroughly convinced that it "would be utterly impossible to secure a jury in the county that would convict Wallis." Public sentiment, he asserted, was that Wallis should be exonerated "for shooting the lecherous wretch Hoyt." A verdict of justifiable homicide, assured Crowley, would not burden the taxpayers of Herkimer Country with a lengthy and costly trial.[162]

As it turned out, Crowley was correct in his estimation of Coroner Strobel. On May 22, at the county courthouse in Herkimer, Strobel rendered his verdict regarding the tragedies that had taken place eighteen days before in Jordanville. He arrived at his verdict of justifiable homicide by using only the testimony of John C. and David Wallis. Hoyt, determined Strobel, had arrived at the Wallis farm in a "drunken condition and in an ugly mood" and, "after having used abusive and violent language towards one, Arvilla Wallis…shot to death and murdered said Arvilla Wallis." After reviewing all the testimony, Coroner Strobel concluded that after the cold-blooded murder of Arvilla, Hoyt then "pointed the revolver in a threatening manner at one John C. Wallis." In short, John C. Wallis had "good and sufficient grounds" to "shoot and kill Ben Hoyt." Not only was he defending himself, recorded Coroner Strobel in his report, but at the same time, Wallis was protecting his father as well. Oddly, he never mentioned the ballistic evidence supplied by officials at Remington Arms.[163]

That same day, the other Strobel, the sheriff, officially discharged John C. Wallis from the Herkimer County Jail. Sheriff Strobel shook hands with Wallis and wished the best of luck to the least troublesome prisoner he had ever housed at the jail. Polite, courteous and grateful for what others had provided him in the jail, John C. Wallis was never locked in his cell. From the county jail, Wallis went to Jordanville with Abram Steele to meet with Town Justice Windsor Maxfield. Steele presented the local magistrate with a copy of Coroner Strobel's report, and after reading the last line of the report, "I therefore order that the said John C. Wallis be discharged," Justice Maxfield rose from his desk and extended his hand to Wallis. The charge of homicide, he informed him, was officially dismissed.[164]

When Wallis walked outside the town hall a free man, he was besieged by well-wishers. "Jordanville Is Jubilant" was how one newspaper reacted. Wallis, observed one reporter, was "deeply touched by the greetings which he received from the folks among whom his life had passed." That night, he slept at the family homestead for the first time since the tragedy.[165] Relieved as he was that the coroner's inquest had ruled that he had acted in self-defense, or carried out a justifiable homicide, his ordeal was not over. The coroner's inquest had exonerated him, but the grand jury had to consider the charge of murder. In the months that led up to the court date, Wallis expressed confidence that the charges against him would be dismissed.

That December, George W. Ward presented the evidence he had gathered to the grand jury, and as almost everyone expected, no indictment was handed down. The testimony provided by Coroner Strobel, together with the autopsy report and the ballistic evidence furnished by the Remington Arms Company, convinced the grand jury that Wallis was justified in his actions.

AFTERWORD

Acquitted by the Herkimer County grand jury, John C. Wallis returned to his farm, cared for his father and took another wife. On June 25, 1902, following a discreet courtship, John C. and Jeanette "Nettie" Mumford were united in marriage at the home of Mortimer and Mary Mumford Purchase. As with his first marriage, there was quite a difference in the age of the betrothed couple. He was fifty-two years old, and that June, she had just celebrated her twenty-fourth birthday. As it turned out, the marriage ceremony was a Mumford family affair, with the bride's sister hosting the wedding, a cousin providing music and a niece serving as a ring bearer, a sister as the maid of honor and a brother as the best man.[166]

While the local press reported the nuptials tastefully by describing how the house was decorated, the bride's dress, the wedding presents that were received and a long list of guests, the *Utica Observer* chose to rehash the double homicide for the benefit of its readers. The paper erroneously recorded that "Hoyt stole up to the house from a hiding place in the barn and, after vain attempts to get the woman to desert her husband, shot her." The dreadful article concluded, saying the couple "have gone to live on the Wallis farm near Jordanville. The tragedy occurred fourteen months ago."[167]

Even in death, the specter of murders could not be escaped. When David E. Wallis died on June 18, 1904, at the age of eighty-seven, the *Herkimer Democrat* followed in the *Utica Observer*'s footsteps. The editors of the paper failed to mention that David was one of the most revered men in the community. He was, in fact, a hardworking farmer who remained active in

The Wallis family plot at Highland Rural Cemetery in Jordanville. *Author's collection.*

many organizations in Jordanville. Instead, the *Democrat* took the same road as the *Utica Observer*. With the banner headline, "D.E. Wallis Dead; Only Eye Witness of Double Shooting in Jordanville," the *Democrat* presented a paragraph-long synopsis of the tragedy, adding only that David E. Wallis "is survived by a son, John."[168]

In 1913, at the age of sixty-three, John C. Wallis retired from farming and moved his family, which included his six-year-old daughter Maria, to Bronner Street in Richfield Springs. He died there on July 31, 1920. His brief obituary in the *Richfield Springs Mercury* never mentioned the events of that fateful May but instead saw the man for who he was. "He was a prosperous farmer and speculator, a good citizen and honest in all his dealings and a firm observer of the golden rule. He leaves to mourn him a wife and daughter who have the sympathy of the entire community."[169] When he was buried at Highland Rural Cemetery in Jordanville, his wife Nettie made sure he was not interred next to first wife, Arvilla.

Nettie survived John C. by forty-five years and was buried in between him and Arvilla. Maria grew up, graduated from Richfield High School and, on October 14, 1923, married Ellis Smith. In her mid-thirties, Maria displayed symptoms of mental illness, suffering from a combination of stress and depression and exhibiting suicidal tendencies. On May 26, 1941, she calmly walked into her living room and announced to her family that she intended to kill herself. While her husband; sixteen-year-old son, Monte; and five-year-old daughter, Marilyn, looked on in horror, she raised a gun to her head. Maria Wallis Smith was buried beside her mother in Highland Cemetery.[170]

Having failed to protect the memory of her late sister, the thrice-married Oretha Crane returned to Kalamazoo, Michigan. It isn't known whether she ever returned to Jordanville or Van Hornesville. If she had, there would have been, in all likelihood, no choir to preach to. The townspeople forgot all about Arvilla and, in some respects, all about John C. Wallis after he moved to Richfield Springs. Oretha Crane died of a cerebral hemorrhage on February 16, 1940, at Van Buren County Hospital in Kendall, Pine Grove, Michigan. She was predeceased by her son from her first marriage, John G. Brown, on December 24. 1939.[171] Like his mother, he, too, was married three times.

After the inquest, Gertie Hoyt moved from Vails Mills to Gloversville. Here, she not only got a job in one of the many leather factories, but she also got a husband. Fred Hulett had served for three years in the army and returned to Gloversville, where he found employment in a glove factory. The two were married on March 14, 1903. By 1920, the couple had relocated to California and found employment as attendants at the Sanoma State Hospital for the Feeble Minded and later the Napa Insane Asylum. Gertie died on September 13, 1959. Her cremated remains were interred at Chapel of the Pines in Los Angeles.[172]

Like his late brother Ben, Andrew Hoyt struggled with alcoholism his entire adult life. In addition to having been arrested for several petty thefts, he was arrested numerous times in Gloversville for public intoxication. Perhaps in an attempt to discipline himself, Andrew Hoyt enlisted in the army on February 24, 1902. He promptly deserted on June 6, 1902, and returned to Gloversville, where he worked for the remainder of his life as a farm laborer. He never married and died on April 19, 1921, at the age of forty-seven. He was buried in Prospect Hill Cemetery in Gloversville.[173]

When Arvilla returned to the farm after her fourteen-month stay in Detroit, she told her ex-husband that there was only one person in Jordanville she did not want to see. At the inquest, John C. Wallis never alluded to who that person might be, but it was a safe bet it was her former lover Samuel Shupe. Arvilla begged him to destroy the love letter she sent him. He never did, and it was used as evidence in her divorce. After working on several farms as a hired man, Samuel Shupe moved to Flint, Michigan, and after a brief stint with the Flint Police Department, he found a job on the assembly line at the Chevrolet Motor Company. On February 12, 1914, he married Alice Elizabeth Burrough Crocker. She divorced him on December 29, 1917, citing "extreme cruelty." Samuel Shupe died on July 25, 1942, from complications of pneumonia and heart disease. He was buried in Northville, Michigan.[174]

The Hoyt-Wallis murder was the highlight of Dan Strobel's three-year term as sheriff. After his tenure, he served as a state committeeman and later served as postmaster in the village of Herkimer, all the while tightening his grip on county politics. The old grass-roots politician loved the caucus and despised the newly introduced primary way of electing one to office. During his second bid to become sheriff of Herkimer County, Strobel found himself against a bevy of candidates, three of whom were his friends. In an effort to thin the primary race between his friends, Strobel suggested they settle the issue over a game of pitch. Strobel won the card game but lost the primary to Leo Lawrence. The colorful party boss of Herkimer County died at the age of eighty-seven on December 31, 1947.[175]

George W. Ward never questioned the findings of the coroner's inquest. In fact, he was probably relieved that they arrived at their verdict. With the anti-Hoyt sentiment displayed at the inquest, Ward knew it would be impossible to get a jury to convict John C. Wallis. The murder trial that Ward was counting on to enhance his political career wouldn't take place until 1906. That was the year Chester Gillette was accused of the bludgeoning and drowning death of his pregnant girlfriend, Grace Brown, at Big Moose Lake. In one of the most celebrated trials in the country, Gillette was found guilty and electrocuted at Auburn Prison, and Ward went on to become a county judge. He fell victim to the Spanish influenza pandemic and died at the age of forty-eight on October 3, 1918.[176]

As for the residents of Jordanville who witnessed the inquest or, in some cases, offered testimony, they accepted the innocence of John C. Wallis. His reputation among his friends wasn't damaged in the least. Most everyone agreed that this was a home invasion, and John C. Wallis acted accordingly. He defended not only his home but also himself and his aged father. The reputation of his ex-wife was another matter. One unexpected consequence of the inquest was how it altered everyone's perception of Arvilla Tunnicliff Wallis. She damned her own memory by her own hand. Her letters, noted one newspaper, proved how adept she was at deceiving everyone. "She showered terms of endearment on Hoyt and wrote love letters to him. She made her own sister believe one thing and Hoyt's relatives believe another. Altogether, she seems to be a past mistress in the art of deception."[177] The *Gloversville Daily Leader* was more blunt: "In the case of the woman, judgment may be reserved, but it inclines to the theory that she was as deep in guilt as Hoyt and deserves little pity for her unhappy end."[178]

NOTES

Chapter 1

1. Hurd, *History of Otsego*, 298–99.
2. 1850 census, Herkimer County, NY.
3. Index of deeds, 2333, mortgage index, 755, Herkimer County Clerk's Office.
4. Eckler, *Eckler Families*, n.p.
5. "Michigan Fever, Part 1," in *Michigan State University Geography Department*, 1–2.
6. Chapman Brothers, *Portrait and Biographical Album*, 277.
7. "Jordanville's Double Tragedy," *Journal and Courier*, May 14, 1901.
8. Reynolds, *History of Southern New York*, 3:1,151.
9. "In Warren," *Journal and Courier*, September 10, 1868.
10. Agricultural record for 1875, census, Herkimer County Clerk's Office.
11. *John C. Wallis v. Wallace Devoe*, Herkimer County Clerk's Office.

Chapter 2

12. "Arvillo Shaul," *Richfield Springs Mercury*, January 10, 1917.
13. "The Hoyt Wallis Tragedy," *Saturday Globe*, May 11, 1901.
14. "What a Lady Friend Has to Say of One of the Victims of the Warren Tragedies," *Little Falls Evening Times*, May 21, 1901; "Wallis Pleads Not Guilty," *Little Falls Evening Times*, May 9, 1901.

15. Ibid.; "Avenged Wife's Murder," *Little Falls Evening Times*, May 6, 1901.
16. "Before the Town Justice," *Little Falls Evening Times*, May 16, 1901; "Some Queer Correspondences," *Gloversville Daily Leader*, May 16, 1901.
17. 1870 Herkimer County census, Bureau of the Census.
18. "What a Lady Friend Has to Say," *Little Falls Evening Times*.
19. "Jordanville," *Herkimer Democrat*, March 26, 1884.
20. "What a Lady Friend Has to Say," *Little Falls Evening Times*.
21. *Wallis v. Wallis* divorce papers, Herkimer County Clerk's Office.
22. Index of deeds, Otsego County Clerk's Office.
23. "Was Not a Forced Marriage," *Little Falls Evening Times*, May 23, 1901.
24. "Jordanville," *Herkimer Democrat*.
25. 1883, index of marriages, vital records, New York State Department of Health (Albany, NY).
26. 1897, death register, vital records, New York State Department of Health (Albany, NY).
27. Death register, clerk, Town of Warren.
28. "Died From Natural Causes," *Otsego Farmer*, January 17, 1898.
29. Ibid.
30. "Avenged," *Little Falls Evening Times*.

Chapter 3

31. 1880, 1890, 1892 Herkimer County census records, Bureau of the Census.
32. "Jordanville," *Ilion Citizen*, March 11, 1898.
33. Death register, clerk, Town of Warren.
34. Michigan marriages, County of Kalamazoo, Michigan Department of Health and Human Services (Lansing, MI), 397.
35. "VanHornsville Notes," *Ilion Citizen*, April 15, 1898.
36. 1900 Herkimer County census.
37. "A Double Tragedy," *Richfield Springs Mercury*, May 9, 1901.
38. *Wallis v. Wallis*, divorce papers, Herkimer County Clerk's Office.
39. *Wallis v. Wallis*, deposition papers, October 16, 1899, Herkimer County Clerk's Office.
40. *Wallis v. Wallis*, Irving Devendorf, October 16, 1899, Herkimer County Clerk's Office.
41. "Inquest at Jordanville," *Evening Times*, May 15, 1901.
42. "Stole His Employer's Wife," *Evening Times*, August 28, 1893.

43. Ibid.

44. DiFonzo and Stern, "Addicted to Fault," 559, 564.

45. *Wallis v. Wallis*, divorce papers, Herkimer County Clerk's Office.

46. Ibid.

Chapter 4

47. Greene, *History*, 3:120–23.

48. *Wallis v. Wallis*, divorce papers, Herkimer County Clerk's Office.

49. *Enlistment of Boys*, 81:58.

50. "Mr. Shupe Disappointed," *Daily Press*, April 22, 1898.

51. *Wallis v. Wallis*, divorce papers, Herkimer County Clerk's Office.

52. *Wallis v. Wallis*, Arvilla Wallis letter, exhibit 1, Herkimer County Clerk's Office.

Chapter 5

53. Letters of administration, estate of Jane Wallis, Herkimer County Surrogate Court.

54. 1900 census, Detroit, MI.

55. "Hoyt Wallis Tragedy," *Saturday Globe*.

56. "Jordanville," *Herkimer Democrat*.

57. "Hoyt Wallis Tragedy," *Saturday Globe*.

58. Parish, *Report of the Women's Christian Temperance Union*, 145.

59. "Mrs. Wallis Feared Hoyt," *Evening Times*, May 10, 1901.

60. *Wallis v. Wallis*, divorce papers, Herkimer County Clerk's Office.

61. "Queer Correspondences," *Gloversville Daily Leader*.

62. "The Hoyt-Wallis Tragedy," *Utica Daily Press*, May 16, 1901.

63. "Told the Story of the Shooting," *Utica Observer*, May 17, 1901.

64. "Jordanville," *Ilion Citizen*.

65. "On the Witness Stand," *Utica Daily Press*, May 10, 1901.

66. "A Small Pox Warning," *New York Evening Post*, January 3, 1901.

67. "Wallis Tells His Story," *Evening Times*, May 17, 1901.

68. "Story of the Shooting," *Utica Observer*.

69. "Witness Stand," *Utica Daily Press*.

Chapter 6

70. "Avenged," *Little Falls Evening Times.*
71. "Wallis Feared Hoyt," *Evening Times.*
72. "The Wallis Tragedy," *Ilion Citizen*, May 17, 1901.
73. Ibid.
74. "Murder in Warren," *West Winfield Star*, May 9, 1901.
75. "Wallis Tragedy," *Ilion Citizen.*
76. "Witness Stand," *Utica Daily Press.*
77. "Wallis Tells His Story," *Evening Times.*
78. "Witness Stand," *Utica Daily Press.*

Chapter 7

79. "County Jail," *Herkimer Democrat*, December 14, 1897.
80. Greene, *History*, 4:422–23; "Was Veteran in Politics," *Evening Telegram*, December 31, 1947; "Statement of the Board of County Canvasses of the County of Herkimer," *Journal and Courier*, December 14, 1897.
81. "A State Issue," *Ilion Citizen*, October 26, 1900.
82. *Herkimer County Board of Supervisors Minutes*, 14–15.
83. "Local Politics," *Utica Sunday Tribune*, July 17, 1910.
84. "Weary Willies Must Work," *Ilion Citizen*, March 21, 1901.
85. "Wallis Loved Wayward Wife," *Utica Sunday Journal*, May 12, 1901.
86. "Avenged," *Little Falls Evening Times.*
87. "A Double Killing," *Otsego Farmer*, May 10, 1901.
88. "Wallis Loved," *Utica Sunday Journal.*
89. Ibid.

Chapter 8

90. "Jealous of Divorced Wife, He Slew Her," *New York Herald*, May 5, 1901.
91. "Shot to Avenge His Erring Wife," *New York Herald*, May 6, 1901.
92. "Because They Loved Her So," *Gloversville Daily Leader*, May 7, 1901.
93. "The Hoyt Wallis Murder," *Utica Observer*, May 6, 1901.
94. "A Horrible Tragedy," *Herkimer Democrat*, May 8, 1901.
95. "Before the Town Justice," *Evening Times.*
96. "John C. Wallis and His Townsmen," *Ilion Citizen*, May 10, 1901.

97. "Murder in Warren," *West Winfield Star*.

98. "Inquest," *Evening Times*.

99. "Avenged," *Little Falls Evening Times*.

100. "Before the Town Justice," *Evening Times*.

101. "They Loved Her," *Gloversville Daily Leader*.

102. "Horrible Tragedy," *Herkimer Democrat*.

103. "Don't Make Love to Another Man's Wife," *Freeman's Journal*, May 9, 1901.

Chapter 9

104. "Death Claims Dr. Strobel," *St. Johnsville Enterprise and News*, July 21, 1937.

105. Hoyt-Wallis Papers, Cathy Hoke interview with Howard King at Jordanville, New York, February 25, 1975, Herkimer County Historical Society.

106. "Hoyt Wallis Murder," *Utica Observer*.

107. "Horrible Tragedy," *Herkimer Democrat*.

108. "Mrs. Wallis Buried Today," *Evening Times*, May 7, 1901.

109. *Herkimer County Board of Supervisors Minutes*, 146.

110. "Deaths Demand," *Fort Plain Standard*, October 10, 1918.

111. "Bravo for the Attorney," *Utica Sunday Tribune*, May 24, 1896.

Chapter 10

112. "William Irving Walter," *Richfield Springs Mercury*, November 10, 1921.

113. "The Man About Town," *Ilion Citizen*, May 31, 1901.

114. "The Man About Town," *Ilion Citizen*, May 17, 1901.

115. "Woman's Sin Not Justified," *Evening Times*, May 25, 1901; "'Thirty' Comes to Newspaper Writer," *Amsterdam Evening Recorder*, July 10, 1918.

116. "Guilty! The Travis-Dykeman Tragedy," *Utica Daily Observer*, May 8, 1874.

117. "The Warren Shooting Affair," *Utica Daily Observer*, December 2, 1870.

118. "Supposed Case of Poisoning in Herkimer County," *Troy Daily Whig*, May 18, 1869.

119. Hopson and Perkins, eds., *Murder and Mayhem in Herkimer*, 27–28.

120. "Wallis Pleads," *Little Falls Evening Times*.

121. Ibid.

122. Ibid.
123. "Wallis Loved," *Utica Sunday Journal*.
124. "Not a Forced Marriage," *Little Falls Evening Times*.
125. Ibid.
126. Ibid.
127. Ibid.

Chapter 11

128. "The Man About Town," *Ilion Citizen, Ilion Citizen*, May 28, 1901; "Inquest," *Evening Times*.
129. "Murder in Warren," *West Winfield Star*.
130. "Witness Stand," *Utica Daily Press*.
131. "Wallis Feared Hoyt," *Evening Times*.
132. "To-Day at Jordanville," *Gloversville Daily Leader*, May 9, 1901.
133. "Wallis Feared Hoyt," *Evening Times*.
134. "Wallis Tells His Story," *Evening Times*.
135. "Wallis Feared Hoyt," *Evening Times*.
136. Ibid.
137. "Double Tragedy," *Little Falls Journal and Courier*.
138. "Queer Correspondences," *Gloversville Daily Leader*.
139. "The Wallis Tragedy," *Ilion Citizen*, May 17, 1901.
140. Ibid.

Chapter 12

141. "Hoyt Wallis Murder," *Utica Observer*.
142. "Double Tragedy," *Little Falls Journal and Courier*.
143. "Hoyt Wallis Tragedy," *Saturday Globe*.
144. "Old Man's Story," *Evening Herald*, May 16, 1901.
145. "Story of the Shooting," *Utica Observer*.
146. "Witness Stand," *Utica Daily Press*.
147. Ibid.
148. "The Hoyt Wallis Tragedy," *Utica Daily Press*, May 16, 1901.
149. Ibid.
150. "Inquest," *Evening Times*.

151. "Before the Town Justice," *Evening Times*.
152. "Wallis Tells His Story," *Evening Times*.
153. Ibid.
154. "Witness Stand," *Utica Daily Press*.
155. Ibid.
156. Hoyt-Wallis Papers, Hoke interview with King; author's interview with Madalyn Shoemaker Juna, spring 1982.

Chapter 13

157. Kling, *Ballistics*, 26–27.
158. "Wallis to Be Set Free," *Johnstown Daily Republican*, May 20, 1901.
159. "The Man About Town," *Ilion Citizen*, May 31, 1901.
160. "The Wallis Case," *Herkimer Democrat*, May 22, 1901.
161. Ibid.
162. "Inquest," *Evening Times*.
163. "Wallis Is Discharged," *Evening Times*, May 22, 1901.
164. Ibid.
165. "Jordanville Is Jubilant," *Gloversville Daily Leader*, May 23, 1901.

Afterword

166. "Wallis-Mumford," *Otsego Farmer*, July 4, 1902.
167. "Takes Another Wife," *Utica Observer*, June 30, 1902.
168. "D.E. Wallis Dead," *Herkimer Democrat*, July 2, 1904.
169. "John C. Wallis," *Richfield Springs Mercury*, August 5, 1920.
170. "Mrs. Ellis M. Smith," *Richfield Springs Mercury*, May 26, 1921.
171. Death Certificate file numbers 80 6751, 80 6676, Michigan Department of Health and Human Services (Lansing, MI).
172. 1903, marriage records, vital records, New York State Department of Health (Albany, NY); 1920, 1930, 1940 California census, Bureau of the Census; death certificate no. 7053 17227, vital records, California Department of Public Health (Sacramento, CA).
173. "Andrew Hoyt," *Morning Herald*, May 17, 1914; "U.S. Army Register of Enlistments 1798–1914," War Department Records (Washington, D.C.), 246–47.

174. Michigan marriage records, no. 1663, Michigan divorce records, County of Genesee no. 7161, Michigan death certificate no. 28216116, Michigan Department of Health and Human Services (Lansing, MI).
175. "Veteran in Politics," *Evening Telegram*.
176. "Death's Demand," *Fort Plain Standard*, October 10, 1918.
177. "Hoyt Wallis Tragedy," *Saturday Globe*.
178. "They Loved Her," *Gloversville Daily Leader*.

BIBLIOGRAPHY

Newspapers

Amsterdam Evening Recorder
Daily Press (Utica, NY)
Evening Herald (Syracuse, NY)
Evening Telegram (Herkimer, NY)
Evening Times (Little Falls, NY)
Fort Plain Standard
Freeman's Journal (Cooperstown, NY)
Gloversville Daily Leader
Herkimer Democrat
Hudson Daily Register
Ilion Citizen
Johnstown Daily Republican
Journal and Courier (Little Falls, NY)
Morning Herald (Gloversville, NY)

New York Evening Post
New York Herald
Otsego Farmer (Cooperstown, NY)
Richfield Springs Mercury
Saturday Globe (Utica, NY)
St. Johnsville Enterprise and News
Troy Daily Whig
Utica Daily Observer
Utica Daily Press
Utica Observer
Utica Sunday Journal
Utica Sunday Tribune
Utica Weekly Herald
West Winfield Star

Primary Sources

Bureau of the Census, Washington, D.C.

Enlistment of Boys in the United States Navy. Vol. 81. Washington, D.C.: War Department Records, n.d.

Estate of Jane Wallis, Herkimer County Surrogate Court Records.

Herkimer County Board of Supervisors Minutes, 1901. Ilion and Herkimer, NY: Citizen Publishing Company, 1902.

Herkimer County Census Records, Herkimer County Clerk's Office.

Herkimer County Jail Records, Herkimer County Clerk's Office.

Hoyt-Wallis Papers. Herkimer County Historical Society.

Index of Deeds, Herkimer County Clerk's Office

Index of Deeds, Otsego County Clerk's Office.

Michigan Department of Health and Human Services (Lansing, MI).

U.S. Army Register of Enlistments 1778–1914. War Department Records (Washington, D.C.).

Vital records. California Department of Public Health (Sacramento, CA).

Vital records. New York State Department of Health (Albany, NY).

Vital statistics. Town of Warren.

Wallis Papers. Herkimer County Clerk's Office.

Wallis v. Wallis divorce papers. Herkimer County Surrogate Court Records.

War Department Records, National Archives

Secondary Sources

Chapman Brothers. *Portrait and Biographical Album of St. Joseph County, Michigan.* Chicago, IL: Chapman Brothers, 1889.

DiFonzo, J. Herbie, and Ruth C. Stern. "Addicted to Fault: Why Divorce Reform Has Lagged in New York." *Pace Law Review* 27, no. 4 (June 2007): 559–64.

Eckler, A. Ross. *Eckler Families of Stark*, privately published, n.d.

Greene, Nelson. *History of the Mohawk Valley.* Vol. 3. Chicago, IL: S.J. Clarke Publishing Company, 1925.

———. *History of the Mohawk Valley.* Vol. 4. Chicago, IL: S.J. Clarke Publishing Company, 1925.

Greiner, James M. *Last Woman Hanged: Roxalana Druse.* Keene, NH: Surry Cottage Books, 2010.

Hopson, Caryl, and Susan Perkins, eds. *Murder and Mayhem in Herkimer County.* Charleston, SC: The History Press, 2019.

Hurd, D. Hamilton. *History of Otsego County, New York.* Philadelphia, PA: Everts and Ferris, 1878.

Kling, Andrew. *Ballistics.* Farmington Mills, MI: Lucent Books, 2008.

Little Falls Directory 1889–1900. Utica, NY: George S. Hughes Publisher, 1900.

Michigan State University Geography Department. *Michigan State University Geography Department.* Lansing: Michigan State University, n.d.

New Century Atlas of Herkimer County. Philadelphia, PA: Century Map Company, 1906.

Parish, Julia R., ed. *25th Annual Report of the Women's Christian Temperance Union.* Bay City, MI: Bay City, 1909.

Reynolds, Cuyler. *Genealogical and Family History of Southern New York and the Hudson River Valley.* Vol. 3. New York: Lewis Historical Publishing Company, 1914.

ABOUT THE AUTHOR

J ames M. Greiner is the Herkimer County historian, a retired high school history teacher and the author of several books and articles on local history. He is the president of the Friends of Historic Herkimer County, an organization working to preserve the Historic 1834 Jail, which once held Roxalana Druse, Chester Gillette and John C. Wallis. He resides in Herkimer, New York, with his wife, Teresa, and their two spoiled dogs, Squirty and Bonnie. He can be reached at jamesmgreiner@gmail.com.